Coaching a Wing-T Based Multiple Offense

Chuck Shroyer

ISBN: 1-58518-949-9
Library of Congress Control Number: 2005936224
Cover design: Jeanne Hamilton
Book layout: Jeanne Hamilton
Diagrams: Deborah Oldenburg
Front cover photo: Brian Bahr/Getty Images

Coaches Choice
P.O. Box 1828
Monterey, CA 93942
www.coacheschoice.com

Dedication/Acknowledgments

To Ron Parks, who as head football coach at Dakota Wesleyan University brought me into his program as a spotter and offensive strategy analyst and valued my offensive input (1973-1978).

To Gordie Fosness, who has been a lifelong encourager of my continuing to develop my coaching career from his positions as DWU's head basketball coach, football defensive coordinator, and athletic director and later heading up South Dakota's Fellowship of Christian Athletes, as well as a strong spiritual advisor (1973-present).

To Dave Wilhelm, who as Southwood (Indiana) High School's head football coach added me to his staff and expanded his offense with many of the ideas presented in this book. We bonded into a unique trusting relationship of offensive coaching efficiency (1994-present).

To Bud Wright, Sheridan (Indiana) High School's head football coach, who repeatedly shared ideas and expertise with me. Bud has won seven state championships, yet is always available to exchange ideas (1984-present).

To Jeff Adamson, Eastbrook (Indiana) High School's head coach, for his coaching friendship, accessibility, sharing ideas, and support as we worked together to improve the football feeder programs for Eastbrook and Blackford High Schools (Indiana) (1990-present).

Contents

The Why and How of the Wing-T Multiple Offense

It is very hard to find the proper talent to run a single-series offense year after year, even if it is a complete series with well-designed plays. Some teams stay with their single sets and do well. Yet, some players look better in one series than others, because some players do certain things better than others. Size, aggressiveness, speed, quickness, toughness, strength, poise, and maturity are all factors. Within a multiple offense with seven series, usually three or four series will fit the team's personnel.

It can be hard to consistently find the right personnel to be successful with a single formation. One example is the I formation. The I formation requires a tailback with very good speed and ruggedness. For success, the I needs a bigger-than-average line, manned by players capable of sustaining their blocks.

On the other hand, a wing-T based multiple offensive system utilizes multiple formations with the backs no deeper than four yards, plus angle block schemes and misdirection that smaller linemen can thrive in. A multiple wing-T offense can also be adjusted to fit the players' attributes, as opposed to trying to make the players fit the offense. In addition, enough variety exists to optimize the available talent. The coaches should be able to find the best position for each player and use the series that fits them best.

Some of the basic premises of the multiple offense package include:

- Two backs in the backfield are necessary to lead for each other, to provide misdirection, to enhance the perimeter attack, to provide better pass blocking, and to complicate the linebacker key reads.
- The wing/slot adds the third quick receiver; runs misdirection tackle traps, counters, and reverses; and blocks for off-tackle and wide plays.
- The wingside tight end is a key receiver, a heavy-duty blocker on the off-tackle plays and the perimeter, and pulls and leads on counter plays.
- Ideally, the end away from the wingside is a flex end, capable of playing both tight and split. He should be the best pass catching end. When aligned tight, he blocks at the point of attack, pulls and leads through the hole when the wing motions to him, and then counters back.
- Wing motion is used to block on the leads, slip into the pass routes, and run tackle traps, counters, and reverses. All of this makes the multiple offense less predictable.
- The threat of the quick pitch and speed option forces the defensive corners to play wider and closer to the line of scrimmage than normal. Thus, they may be vulnerable on deep pass routes.
- Quick dives change the tempo from the somewhat slower lead plays. Usually, one or the other is more successful, and one serves as a change-up for the other.
- The strong sets present a dilemma for the defense. If they shift or slant strong, they can be vulnerable to the counter weak and other plays to the weakside.
- Play-action passes off of the best running plays are the cornerstone of the passing game.
- Three-step dropback passing, plus a few quick play-action passes, are needed to combat blitzing.
- Five-step passes are needed for long-yardage and come-from-behind situations.

Simplifying the Multiple Wing-T Offense

Once again, it is not necessary to run all series. Choose only those that fit the personnel available. Each year, only some of the same series will be run. While some will be dropped, others will be added, because the personnel is different. This change in series should also complicate the opponent's defensive preparation, because they can't simply say, "Oh, we know what they run."

It is important that the line knows the color call is for the backs and only the hole number and name is needed for good line play. The play name describes the blocking. And, those names are the same for all the colors. For example, blasts, counters, or tackle traps are blocked the same, regardless of what color is called.

It is important that the backs know the color call is a road map for them to run the play. For each specific color, they initially do the same action each time. The basic backfield actions for each series are as follows:

Black—The fullback fakes the trap up the middle or carries on 31/32 Trap. The halfback fakes the sweep through the fullback's position or carries on the 27/28 Sweep. The quarterback opens, using the midline technique, looks toward the halfback, fakes or gives to the fullback, fakes or gives to the halfback, and then bootlegs opposite the halfback's direction.

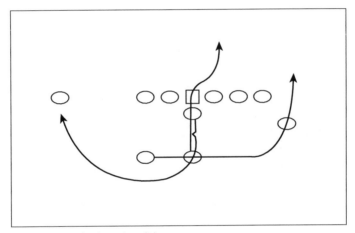

Figure 1-1. Black series (R)

Blue—The fullback arcs to the hole or fakes a 33/34 Belly. The halfback leads through the hole called. The quarterback reverse pivots and fakes or gives to the fullback, drops back, and sets up for the pass.

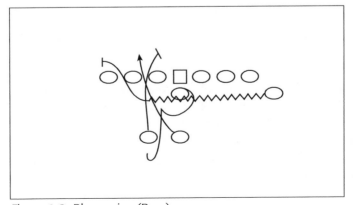

Figure 1-2. Blue series (Ram)

Green—The fullback arcs to the hole or fakes a 33/34 Belly versus the 4-3 and 4-4 or 35/36 Belly versus the 5-2 and 5-3. The halfback, using a one-step motion, fakes an option pitch route towards the wingside. The quarterback reverse pivots and fakes or gives to the fullback on 33/34X or 35/36G and fakes or runs the option versus the called defender.

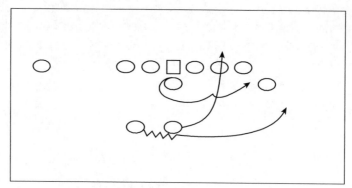

Figure 1-3. Green series (R)

Red—The fullback slants for the guard's outside foot on 33/34 Dive. He will fake if 25/26 Belly, Follow, or Keep is called. The halfback fakes the belly through the fullback's position on 33/34 Dive and 25/26 Follow or Keep, and will carry through the 5/6 hole on 25/26 Belly. The quarterback takes a 45-degree step back and gives or fakes on a 33/34 Dive. He steps back 45 degrees to give on 25/26 Belly, Follow, or Keep.

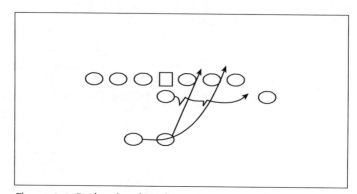

Figure 1-4. Red series (Ram)

The fullback runs 35/36 Belly if called. He will fake on 23/24 Dive, 35/36 Follow, and Keep. Run Red option if called and fake on 25/26 Dive. The halfback fakes 23/24 Dive or carries. The halfback aims at the tackle's back, then veers out to the 5/6 hole on 25/26 Dive. The quarterback steps straight down the line toward the mesh with the halfback. He will give or fake to the halfback and then attack the option man. He angles back to give to the fullback on 35/36 Belly.

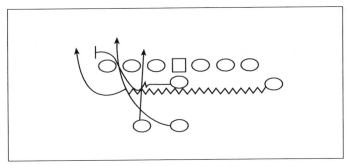

Figure 1-5. Red series (Ram, kick motion)

Orange—The fullback lead blocks through the hole called and looks for the playside inside linebacker. An exception is on 25/26 Power he will run an inside out arc on the defensive end and block him out. The halfback receives the handoff and runs through the hole called. The quarterback reverse pivots toward the halfback, to give him the running lane, and then hands off or fakes. He then hides the ball on his outside hip and runs around the strongside on a bootleg or drops back on an Orange pass.

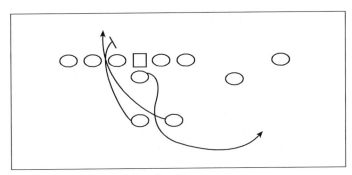

Figure 1-6. Orange series (Rex)

White—The fullback takes two steps toward the halfback, then cuts to the weak guard's outside foot while faking or carrying on 33/34X or 33/34 Fold or 35/36 Fold. The halfback fakes receiving the pitch to the side he's aligned or carries on all plays. The quarterback reverse pivots and pitches or fakes the pitch. If he fakes, he will hand off to the fullback or inside to the wing on the 41/42 Tackle Trap.

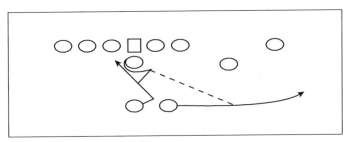

Figure 1-7. White series (Rex)

Gray—The fullback sprints wide looking for the option pitch or fakes receiving the pitch on 41/42 Tackle Trap. The halfback swings wide as the lead blocker on the option or fakes as the lead blocker on all other plays. The quarterback steps back and out with a big 45-degree step to the playside, then angles closer to the line of scrimmage to option the designated man, or hands off inside to the wing on 41/42 Tackle Trap.

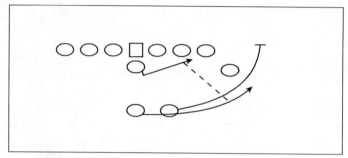

Figure 1-8. Gray series (Sword)

Brown—This series is the same as red when the fullback runs or fakes 33/34 dive. The fullback carries over the guard on 33/34 Blast or fakes on Belly, Crossbuck, or Cross Option. He aims for the tackle and carries on RT/LT Tackle and aims directly at the center on 30 Fan. The playside halfback lead blocks the middle or playside inside linebacker on 33/34 Blast and 30 Fan. He blocks out on the end on Belly RT/LT and 45/26 Crossbuck. When 45/26 Crossbuck-G is called, he leads through the hole and blocks the inside linebacker. He lead blocks on the cross option. The offside halfback fakes the option on 33/34 Blast and RT/LT Tackle. He curves through the hole and carries on Belly RT/LT and 45/26 Crossblock. He sprints through the fullback's position and runs the option pitch on cross option. He lead blocks on the inside linebacker on 30 Fan.

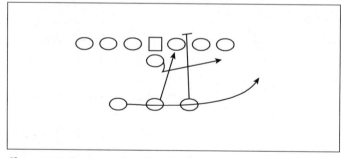

Figure 1-9. Brown series (Jumbo)

Personal Requirements

A brief description of the eight series in the multiple wing-T and the type of talent needed for each position follows. Emphasis is placed on the minimum requirements for each position.

Black—Size of the fullback is less important than toughness and quickness. Speed and quickness in the halfback position are a real bonus. Usually the number two halfback is the wing, and he should have good speed and toughness and catch well. The wing can be a little smaller than the halfback. The line can be of average size, but needs quickness. The guards should be very quick. The quarterback should be a versatile runner/passer.

Blue—A big and tough fullback is ideal. The halfback should be a good blocker with decent size and above average speed. The line should be bigger than in the Black series. With a double-team inside the hole on most plays, size requirements are not excessive. The quarterback should be able to execute play-action passes with a fake, drop back three steps, and set up.

Green—Personnel requirements are similar to the Black series, except the fullback needs more size to pound away on 33/34X and 35/36G. The quarterback should be able to run the double option.

Red—The fullback and halfback only need average speed. Their alignment depth can be adjusted so they hit the hole quickly. The quarterback should be quick, a good ball handler/faker, and good on the double option and the keep. Line requirements are similar to the Blue series.

Orange—This series is a disguised I formation. The fullback needs I fullback blocking skills, and the halfback needs I tailback skills. The quarterback should be able to run the bootleg. The line requirements are like the Black series.

White—The fullback is the same as in the Black series. The halfback should be quick and tough, but can be quite small. The quarterback should be able to make a good pitch, hand off to the wing or the fullback, and fake pitch and pass down the field 15 yards. The line requirements are similar to Black, but the tackles should be quick enough to pull.

Gray—The fullback should have above average speed, agility, and hands. The halfback requirements are the same as the Blue series, but not as much size is required. The quarterback should be able to run the double option; fake and hand off to the wing; and fake option, pull up, and throw the 10-yard dump pass. The line requirements are similar to the Black series.

Brown—The personnel requirements are the same as the Red series.

Simplifying Nomenclature

The goal is to shorten and simplify the verbage used to designate a formation, series, or play call. Thus, a one-syllable word is used for the formation, and the direction of the formation is combined into the name of the formation. Examples of simplified formations and direction of formation include:

R—wing right split left

L—wing left split right

RN—wing right split left nasty (three to five yards flex end split)

LN—wing left split right nasty (three to five yards flex end split)

Ram—wing right tight left

Lion—wing left tight right

Sword—strong wing right

Lance—strong wing left

Rex—strong slot right

Lou—strong slot left

East—pro slot right

West—pro slot left

Jumbo—full house T with special personnel

Examples of series include:

Black—wing-T 20 series

Blue—variation wing-T 80 series

Green—wing-T 80 down series

Orange—wing-T 30 series strong

Red—quick veer dive series

White—quick pitch series

Gray—speed option series

Brown—goal line series (Red variation)

The Cadence

The quarterback should allow the line to align, space, and rest their hands on their knees. The quarterback then calls, "Down," and all linemen go into a three-point stance. He waits until they have been motionless for one second and calls, "Set." The set call starts any motion. Then, he uses a series of three go's. The snap is usually on one of the three go's. Occasionally, the snap will be on set as a surprise, assuming no motion is called. The quarterback also has two ways to have the ball snapped while the line is in a two-point stance. The first is a goose of the center to have the ball snapped silently; the second is to make an "on down" call in the huddle.

The Use of Motion

To eliminate a variable, the snap count is standardized when using motion. Motion should be communicated to the whole team. The scheme may vary from year to year, but, in general, short motion is on one, medium motion is on two, and long motion is on three.

Flipping the Line

The following are simple guidelines to use if flip-flopping the line, the ends, the fullback with the halfback, or the halfback with the wing.

- With a designated strongside/weakside, use strong right as the standard. The line will always align strong right when no call is given. When a "flip" is added to the call, it means strong left.
- When flipping the tight end and flex end, have the tight end always go with the wing/flanker, unless Rex/Lou is called. That way, no call is ever needed.
- If the line doesn't flip, use the word "flip" for the fullback and the halfback to switch. If flip is used for the line, use "switch" for the fullback and halfback exchange.
- To exchange the halfback and wing/slot, use the word "swap."

Teaching the Multiple Offense

The coach should evaluate each player's talent and compare it with the analysis of talents needed for each series covered earlier in this chapter. Decide what series seem logical for the talent available and decide on the sequence of introduction, i.e., what series is to be taught first, second, third, etc.

When introducing a series, put in all the plays from that series, including the passes. That way, it all ties together, and the players see the sequence of plays with the wing/slot and ends getting involved directly with plays in which they play a key role. After two series have been put in, it is beneficial to have a review practice for those two series. After a review practice, add a third series. At a succeeding practice, add a fourth. And then, at the next practice, review the third and fourth series.

The plan for teaching these series should include running each play in a series versus an odd and even defensive front. Decide which defenses to run against based on the majority of odd and even defenses used by your opponents.

One approach is to teach the entire series versus either an even or odd defense. Then, start from the beginning versus the other defense. The other approach is to teach each play versus both an odd and even defense.

How many series to install will depend on how many series the coach decides he can teach and on how well the players can learn and retain. It is possible to add a series or two at mid-season or when preparing for the playoffs. However, it should probably include the smaller series in terms of number of plays. Following is the recommended teaching progression of each series, in descending order of complexity:

- Black
- Blue
- Red
- Brown
- Orange and Green
- White
- Gray

Using the Multiple Offense in Games

Play scripting is suggested to avoid the awkward realization that at halftime the coach hasn't tried three of his six series. Without running a play or two from each series, it is difficult to decide what worked in the first half and what should be emphasized in the second half. Thus, it is best to script at least two plays from each series in the first half and run them to see how they worked. The second half play calling can be planned on those first half observations.

Don't assume that because a team shuts down the first two or three series, that they can stop all the rest of the offense. Usually, their defense has a prepared scheme to stop the best plays versus the last two opponents. If their plan is good and their personnel executes well, they may well make it hard to run what has been good in recent games. But, they probably haven't had the time to prepare for all the series in the multiple offense. Thus, by trying plays from all the series, surprise yardage from some of the series will result from plays not used much in earlier games.

Also, do not assume that a defense doing a good job of stopping the base plays can do the same job of stopping the misdirection plays off the faking of the base plays. By overcommitting to the base plays, they may leave themselves more vulnerable to the counters and tackle traps. And, if they are stopping the base running plays, they may be achieving that by aggressive assistance from their secondary. Hence, play-action passes may be able to exploit the defensive backs.

An analysis of the opponent's defensive personnel is important. Are they big and strong? Are they average size or even smaller? Are they fast, average, or below average in speed? If matched by equal size, strength, and toughness, the defense may be able to stop the Blue, Orange, and Red series. If the defense is not as agile or as quick as the offense, the Black, White, and Gray series with fast hitting plays to the outside and misdirection plays should be more successful.

While nothing is etched in stone, the Blue, Black, and White are base series. Red is used like a baseball pitcher's change-up. Red's lightning fast dives contrast with lead plays, which, while quick, can't match Red's pace. Orange is a valuable supplemental series. Green is in that same category, but could be a base series if the fullback is a real threat and the quarterback can run the option well. Gray is an auxiliary series and a valuable one. If their defensive line has the edge, base runs will be slowed up. Gray will run them sideline to sideline, with an option on the perimeter man who is hardest to block.

In summary, try some form of scripting of play calls. This planning will insure that, sometime in the first half, at least two plays from each series chosen for that game will be run and the results of those plays recorded. Then, in the halftime strategy session, the coach is better prepared to decide what series to emphasize in the critical third and fourth quarters.

2

The System

Understanding the system is key to learning the multiple offense. All nomenclature is streamlined to assist the coaches with teaching and the players with learning.

Hole Numbering System

Refer to Figure 2-1. O means over the center. Gaps to the right are 2, 4, 6, and 8, and gaps to the left are 1, 3, 5, and 7.

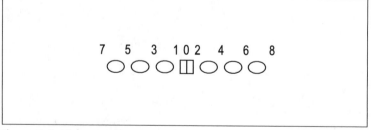

Figure 2-1. Hole numbers

Backfield and Receiver Numbering System

Refer to Figure 2-2.

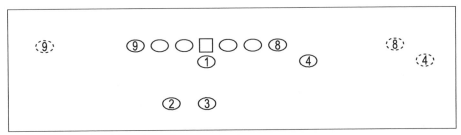

Figure 2-2. Backfield and receiver numbering

The Cadence

The line and backs take their proper alignment and standard spacing and then assume a two-point hands on knees stance. The quarterback will call, "Down," and all players assume a three-point stance. After at least a one-second pause, the quarterback calls, "Set," which starts any called motion. Plays can also start on set, if called in the huddle. The quarterback calls, "Go," and the ball is snapped if "on one" is called in the huddle. The quarterback calls the second go, and the ball is snapped if "on two" is called in the huddle. The quarterback calls the third go, and the ball is snapped if "on three" is called in the huddle. When the line initially takes its stance and assumes a pre-snap two-point stance, the quarterback could have the ball snapped silently on goose or "on down" if called in the huddle.

Formations

To avoid excess verbalizing, traditional words like wing, slot, strong, split, and tight are streamlined into one-syllable words; otherwise, up to three or four words would be required. These carefully paired one-syllable words mean both alignment and strength.

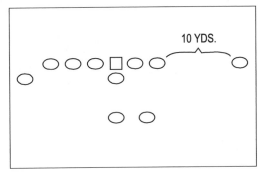

Figure 2-3. L

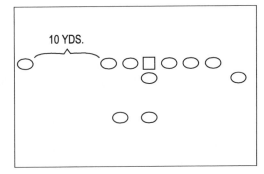

Figure 2-4. R

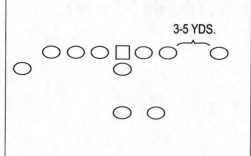

Figure 2-5. LN

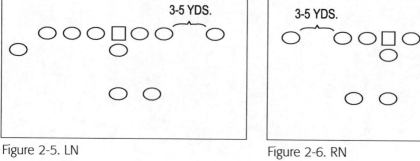

Figure 2-6. RN

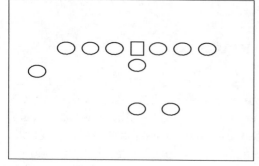

Figure 2-7. Lion

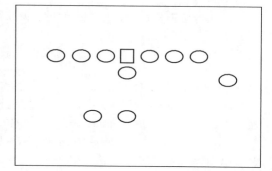

Figure 2-8. Ram

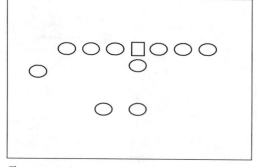

Figure 2-9. Lance

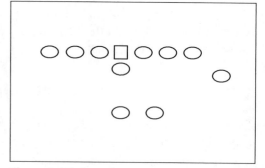

Figure 2-10. Sword

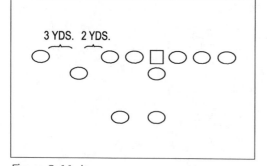

Figure 2-11. Lou

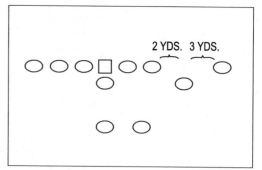

Figure 2-12. Rex

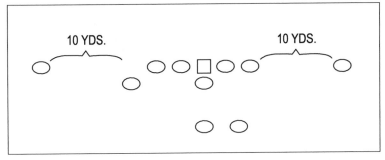

Figure 2-13. West

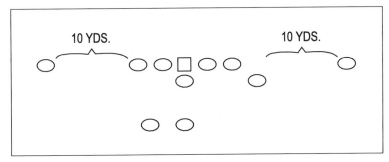

Figure 2-14. East

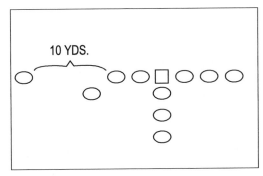

Figure 2-15. I Liz

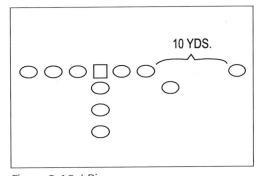

Figure 2-16. I Rip

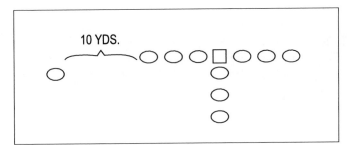

Figure 2-17. I Left

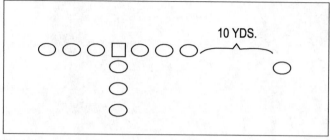

Figure 2-18. I Right

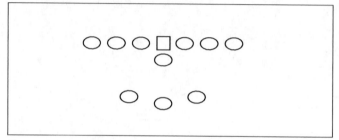

Figure 2-19. Jumbo

Motion

Kick—The wing goes in fast motion, slows as he tags the quarterback, then turns up into the guard/tackle gap and blocks out on the defensive end. The snap count is on one.

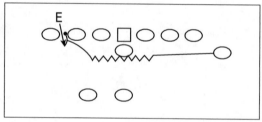

Figure 2-20. Kick motion

Crack—The wing uses the same motion as kick, but maintains speed until wide of the end, then he will either run a pass route, block in on the defensive end or outside linebacker, or turn back to carry on 41/42 Tackle Trap or 45/46 Counter. The snap count is on two.

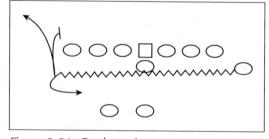

Figure 2-21. Crack motion

Pro—The wing motions outside to make a pro formation. Used with R/L formation. The snap count is on two.

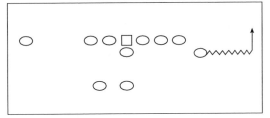

Figure 2-22. Pro motion

Mo—The fullback motions outside the end by stepping forward, then in front of the halfback, and then blocks the defensive end or outside linebacker on white pitch. The snap count is on one.

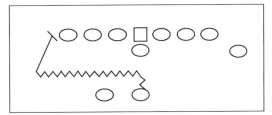

Figure 2-23. Mo motion

Play Calling

The colors not only tell the team what series is being run, but also give the backs the backfield action. This feature will become clearer as each series is studied in more detail.

The sequence of play calling includes: first, formation; second, motion; third, series color; fourth, play name and back and hole number. The play names are descriptive enough to remind the linemen of their blocking assignment (for example, R Black 32 Trap, Lion Kick Blue 34 Blast, East Red 23 Dive, Ram Crack White Pitch Lt.).

Each play should be taught versus an odd and an even defense, i.e., 4-4 and 5-3. The 4-3 is not a big adjustment from the 4-4. Likewise, a 5-2 is not a significant adjustment from 5-3. It's easier to go from expecting more linebackers and adjust to one less than vice versa. But, each play in this text will also be diagrammed versus a 4-3 and 5-2 to offer a complete presentation. While each of the four defensive fronts have many variations, Figures 2-24 through 2-27 present the most common base looks. Versus a split end, the defenders will probably adjust as illustrated in Figures 2-28 through 2-31.

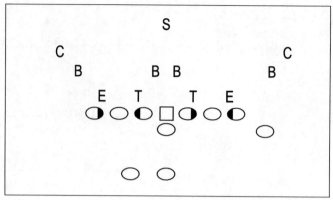

Figure 2-24. 4-4

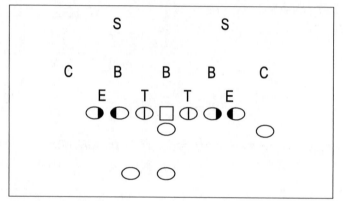

Figure 2-25. 4-3

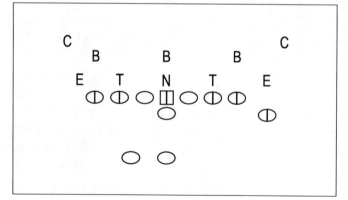

Figure 2-26. 5-3

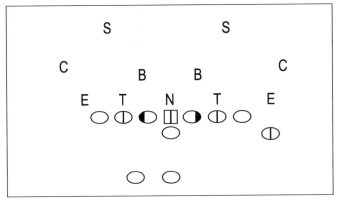

Figure 2-27. 5-2

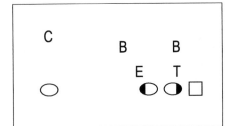

Figure 2-28. 4-4

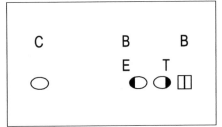

Figure 2-29. 4-3

Figure 2-30. 5-3

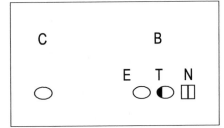

Figure 2-31. 5-2

3

Black Series

Black is the wing-T 20 series. Basic backfield action includes:

Fullback—He is the ballcarrier on 31/32 Trap. Otherwise, he fakes the 31/32 Trap.

Halfback—He is the ballcarrier on 27/28 Sweep. Otherwise, he fakes the sweep.

Quarterback—He hands off to the fullback or empty hand fakes to the fullback and hands off to the halfback and fakes a bootleg. Or, he makes a good ball fake and boots out to the halfback's original side to pass (called boot) or to keep (called bootleg).

The quarterback gives the midline to the fullback (minimizing the curving route the fullback takes on the 31/32 Trap). The quarterback should open to the halfback by taking a 45-degree drop step with the foot away from the halfback, then swing the forward foot straightback towards the halfback at 90 degrees, while moving backwards. The halfback aligns behind the tackle and should remember to randomly do so when other series are called. The essence of learning Black is for each back to learn the above, plus listen for the play call to know who is carrying and who is faking. A key to all series, but especially important to Black, is that all fakes be carried out.

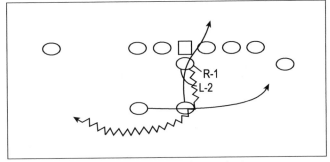

Figure 3-1. Quarterback's footwork on Black

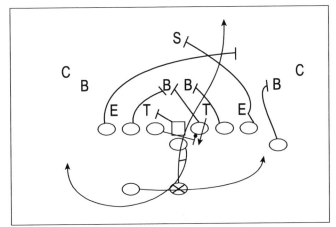

Figure 3-2. Ram Black 32 Trap versus 4-4

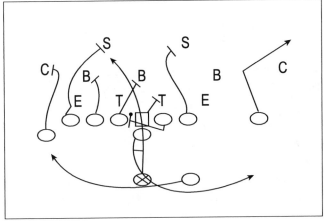

Figure 3-3. L Black 31 Trap versus 4-3

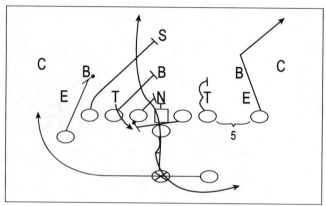

Figure 3-4. LN Black 31 Trap versus 5-3

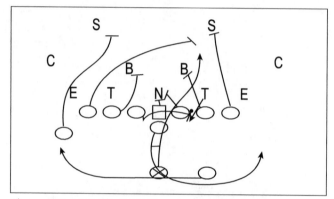

Figure 3-5. Lion Black 32 Trap versus 5-2

End Blocking Rules

If the wing is on a player's side or motioning to him, block the safety. If the defensive end is on his inside shoulder, he should fake block by firing at the end, then shove off before going to the safety. If the wing is away from the player, he should determine if the outside linebacker is over him. If yes, block the linebacker out. If the linebacker is definitely outside of him (like 4-4 outside linebacker), he should block the safety.

Flex end—If split, he should run the V corner pass route. If tight, he should wall off the far cornerback versus a three-deep secondary or block playside safety versus a two-deep secondary.

This play is not ideal for short yardage, because, if the inside linebackers stunt inside, they can plug up the hole. But, inside plugging linebackers will weaken the defense's perimeter defense. Thus, view this play as a potential home run play and expect and tolerate some strike outs.

Two Special Black up the Middle Plays: 30 Fold and 30 Wedge

Both of these plays look like the 31/32 Trap, but no trap action is used. Versus the 5-2 or 5-3 defense, the Ram/Lion Black 30 Fold play is a good alternative to the 31/32 Trap.

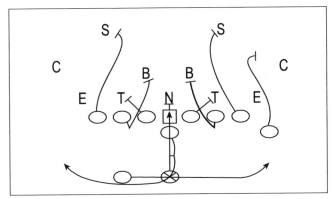

Figure 3-6. Ram Black 30 Fold versus 5-2

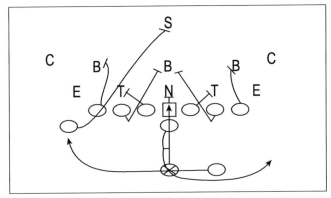

Figure 3-7. Lion Black 30 Fold versus 5-3

Ram/Lion is preferred because they are balanced formations with two tight ends. This formation precludes the possibility of the defense reducing or overshifting their front. The center blocks the nose tackle the easiest way, and the fullback reads the block and breaks to daylight.

Versus the 4-4 or 4-3 defenses, the 30 Wedge play is a good alternative to the 31/32 Trap. The guards widen their split with the center, and the tackles narrow the split with the guards. Versus the 4-4, the guards chip the defensive tackle on their way to block the linebackers. The center and guards zone block the middle creating three blockers on the two linebackers. Versus the 4-3, the guards and tackles double-team the defensive tackles and the fullback reads the center's block on the middle linebacker.

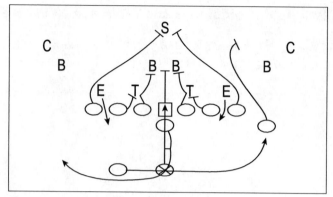

Figure 3-8. Ram Black 30 Wedge versus 4-4

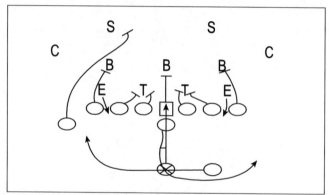

Figure 3-9. Lion Black 30 Wedge versus 4-3

Black 27/28 Sweep

Tight end and wing—The tight end and wing are responsible for the defensive end and the playside inside linebacker. If the defensive end is on the tight end's inside shoulder, he blocks the defensive end and the wing blocks the middle linebacker (4-4 alignment). If the defensive end is wider than head-up on the tight end, the tight end and wing combo block him (5-3 alignment). When the middle linebacker approaches, the tight end leaves the combo to wall off the middle linebacker.

Pulling guards—The playside guard should expect the outside linebacker (or cornerback) to fire up fast to contain the play. If so, he blocks that defender out. If no one fires up, he runs for the corner, but doesn't block until someone tries to cross his face. The backside guard should read the playside guard's reaction to the defense. If the playside guard blocks the contain defender, he should turn up inside that block and look for the safety or backside linebacker. If the playside guard arcs wide like the pitch, he should stay with the guard and not turn up and lead until he blocks.

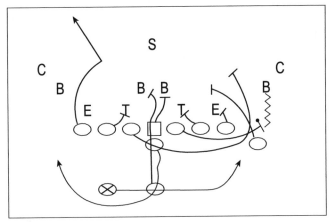

Figure 3-10. Ram Black 28 Sweep versus 4-4

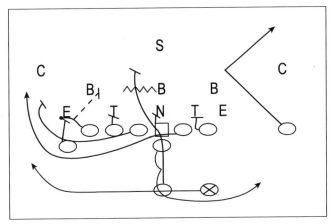

Figure 3-11. L Black 27 Sweep versus 5-3

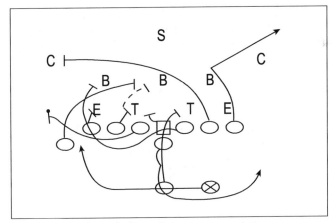

Figure 3-12. Lion Black 27 Sweep versus 4-3

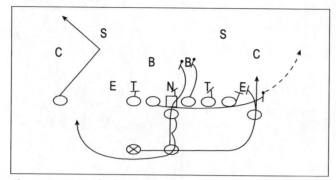

Figure 3-13. R Black 28 Sweep versus 5-2

Versus the 4-3, the wing checks the tight end's block on the defensive end, then blocks the middle linebacker. Versus the 4-4, the wing has the inside linebacker and the backside guard pulls through and blocks the outside linebacker. The playside tackle blocks down on the defensive tackle. If the defensive tackle pinches, he will then block the middle linebacker, and the center will block the defensive tackle as he steps to the playside A gap. The fullback will cut off the backside defensive tackle, and the backside tackle blocks out on the playside cornerback.

Versus the 5-2, the tight end and wing double-team the defensive end. The playside guard should not pull, but cut off the linebacker over him. The backside guard will block out or run an arcing route downfield.

Black 25/26 Trap

A defense may be able to take away the 27/28 Sweep by a wide/containing defensive end alignment, usually some version of 5-2, 5-3, 6-1, or 6-2. Black 25/26 Trap will take advantage of these defenses. The playside tight end and tackle double-team the tackle, the playside guard blocks over, and the backside guard pulls and traps the end. The quarterback slows after faking to the fullback to give the halfback a better angle to hit the 5/6 hole.

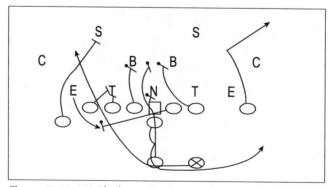

Figure 3-14. LN Black 25 Trap versus 5-2

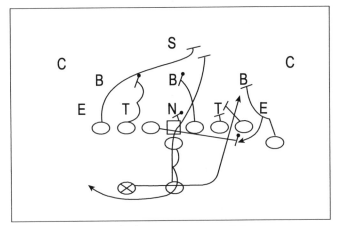

Figure 3-15. Ram Black 26 Trap versus 5-3

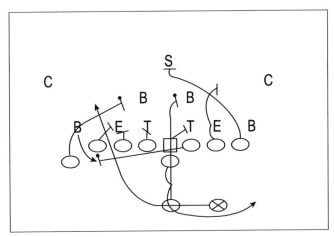

Figure 3-16. Lion Black 25 Trap versus 6-2

Black 45/46 Counter

Black 45/46 is the wing-T counter crisscross. Like the 25/26 Trap, the 45/46 Counter is effective versus the 5-2 and 5-3 defenses. The contain defensive ends are more easily blocked out than to reach block them in an effort to run wide. The fullback curves his trap fake playside to become a key blocker. The wing needs to take a delay step so that he doesn't rush the double handoff. The handoff from the halfback to the wing is an inside handoff. Versus defensive ends aligned on the inside shoulder of the tight ends, the 47/48 Reverse is a good misdirection play. Note the quarterback's key downfield block on the cornerback.

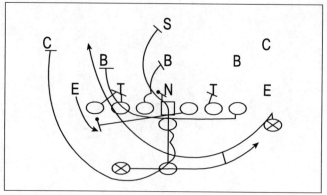

Figure 3-17. Ram Black 45 Counter versus 5-3

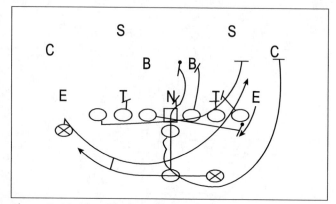

Figure 3-18. Lion Black 46 Counter versus 5-2

Black 47/48 Reverse

Versus 4-4 and 4-3 defenses, with defensive ends aligned tighter, a good call is to run the 47/48 Reverse. The wing's reverse pivot provides the necessary delay to avoid

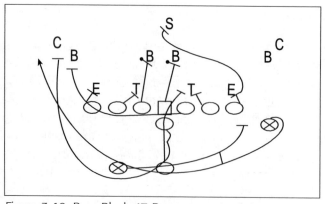

Figure 3-19. Ram Black 47 Reverse versus 4-4

rushing the double handoff. The fullback fills for the pulling guard, as does the backside tackle versus both the 4-4 and the 4-3 defenses. The quarterback lead blocks on the first unblocked defender he encounters on both Black Counter and Reverse.

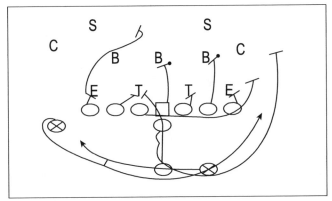

Figure 3-20. Lion Black 48 Reverse versus 4-3

Black Bootleg

For clarification, boot means boot pass and bootleg means the quarterback makes it look like boot, but keeps the ball and runs. Two bootlegs exist. Bootleg from the Ram/Lion, R/L, and RN/LN formations goes to the flex end side. The Sword/Lance and Rex/Lou bootlegs go to the wingside. The blocking for these two bootlegs are identical, except an extra blocker exists on the wingside. If the defense is a 4-4 or a 4-3, either bootleg is good. Versus contain defensive ends (5-3, 5-3, 6-2), to bootleg to the flex end side, use RN/LN formation. Otherwise, bootleg to the wing.

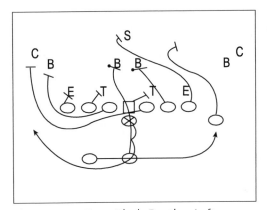

Figure 3-21. Ram Black Bootleg Left versus 4-4

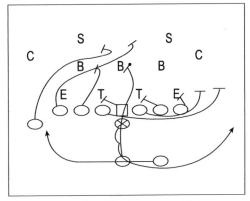

Figure 3-22. Lion Black Bootleg Right versus 4-3

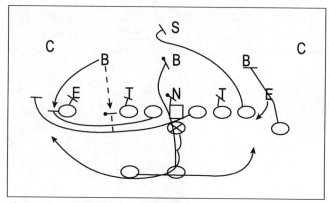

Figure 3-23. RN Black Bootleg Left versus 5-3

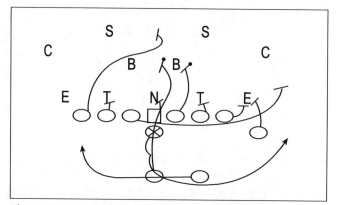

Figure 3-24. Sword Black Bootleg Right versus 5-2

Black Boot

This pass play is excellent when the defense reads 31/32 Trap, 27/28 Sweep, or Bootleg. If the defense does read pass, they have four receivers to try to cover. Finally, if the quarterback isn't contained and is unsure of the pass, he should keep and run for the easy yards.

Flex end—Bluffs the stalk block on the outside linebacker and runs a corner route.

Fullback—Fakes the trap through the playside A gap and blocks any linebacker stunt. If no linebacker stunts, run a seven-yard out.

Tight end—Runs across at 12-yards deep over the flex end's aligned spot. Versus two deep, splits the safeties.

Wing—Runs a seven to eight-yard square in.

Onside guard—Pulls for depth to hook the defensive end.

Center—Steps to the backside A gap, watches for a linebacker stunt, and helps the tackle if needed.

Quarterback—Rolls out deep, reads the #1 through #4 receivers, and throws to the most open receiver. If all receivers are covered, keep and run outside. If no contain shows, fakes the pass and runs outside.

Flex end—When split, runs a post corner route.

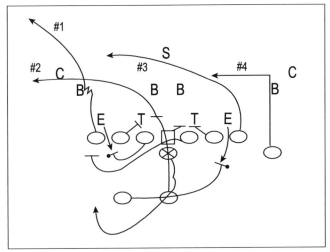

Figure 3-25. Ram Black Boot Left versus 4-4

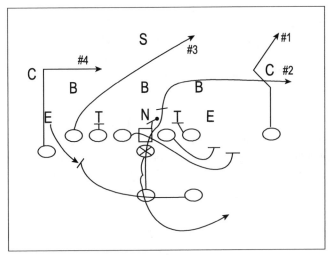

Figure 3-26. L Black Boot Right versus 5-3

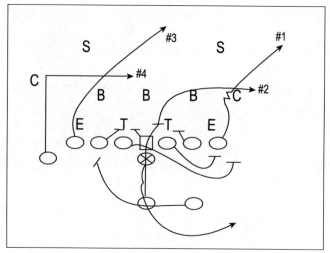

Figure 3-27. Lion Black Boot Right versus 4-3

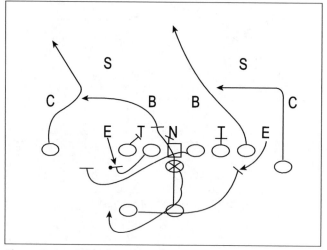

Figure 3-28. R Black Boot Left versus 5-2

Black Boot—Switch

After running the boot repeatedly, a change-up route is needed to keep the defense honest. For simplicity, switch tells the flex end to run a comeback route, the fullback to run a corner route, and the tight end and wing to occupy the safety and the backside cornerback. No change in blocking occurs. But, a reduced defensive tackle forces the guard to block him and the tackle to block the defensive end.

The first time a switch is run in each game, alert the quarterback to key the safety and throw opposite his reaction. This change-up will probably force the safety to cover the fullback, thus the quarterback should read the split end or the tight end for the open receiver. For simplicity of comparison, Boot Switch is only shown from R, but it is equally effective from L. It may be good strategy to run it from the opposite formation the second time it is run in a game.

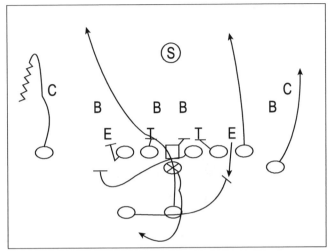

Figure 3-29. R Black Boot Switch versus three deep

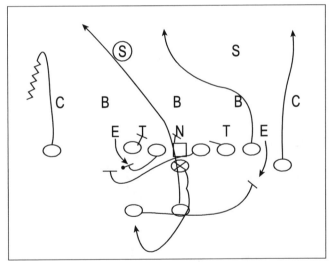

Figure 3-30. R Black Boot Switch versus two deep

Black Boot from Strong Set

The blocking from Sword and Lance formations is identical on Black Boot from Ram/Lion versus all defenses, except that the tight end and wing exchange assignments and routes on the fours and the fives.

Tight End—Slams the defensive end, versus the fours, and then runs a seven-yard out route. Versus the fives, the tight end bluffs a block on the outside linebacker and then runs a corner route.

Wing—Slams the defensive end versus the fives and then runs a seven-yard out route. Versus the fours, runs to fake a block on the linebacker, then runs a V out route.

Fullback—Runs the standard boot, except throttles down when open to keep the spacing with the wider receiver in the flat.

Flex end—Runs an across route aiming for 12-yard depth over the tight end's original alignment.

All routes are identical except the flex end's route changes from an across versus a three deep to split the safeties versus a two deep. No switch route exists for Strong Black Boot.

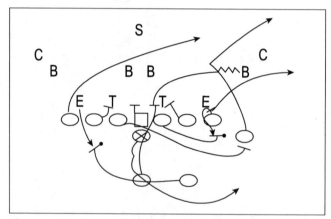

Figure 3-31. Sword Black Boot Right versus 4-4

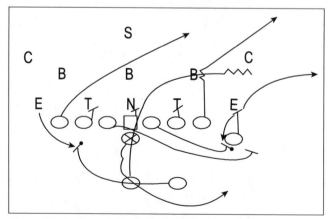

Figure 3-32. Sword Black Boot Right versus 5-3

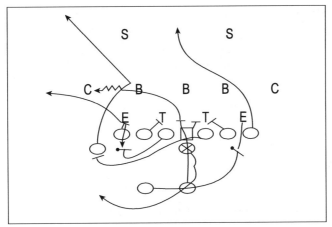

Figure 3-33. Lance Black Boot Left versus 4-3

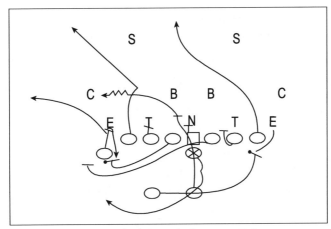

Figure 3-34. Lance Black Boot Left versus 5-2

Black Screen

This screen is blocked the same versus all defenses and from all formations.

Halfback—Blocks the end hard, then slides off toward the line, deepens, and sets up facing the quarterback.

Fullback—Curves through A gap away from screenside and blocks any penetration. If none, runs a seven-yard decoy out route.

Center, playside guard, and tackle—Sets up and shows Black pass for three counts, then releases outside. The tackle aims for a spot six yards wider than the original tight end spot. The guard aims for a spot two yards inside the tackle, and the center aims for a spot two yards inside the guard. As soon as the halfback catches the ball, he yells, "Go," and the three screen blockers lead him down the field.

When the defensive tackle aligns inside the guard to the split end side, the guard stays and blocks the defensive tackle and the tackle blocks the defensive end. Otherwise, the tackle blocks down on the defensive tackle and the guard pulls away from the screen side and hook blocks E. Tips for running effective screens:

- The quarterback's pass should be slightly upfield so the halfback can catch it and go forward with momentum.
- The quarterback's depth should be deeper than normal.
- The quarterback should look at his decoy receivers before turning and passing to the halfback.
- Decoy receivers should run hard to fool the secondary.
- Any lineman who has a man to block should do so aggressively.
- Once the halfback has the ball, he should start straight upfield for as long as possible and then break outside.
- The R/L and Ram/Lion screens attack the strong (wing and tight end) side, while Sword/Lance screen attacks the weak (flex end) side.

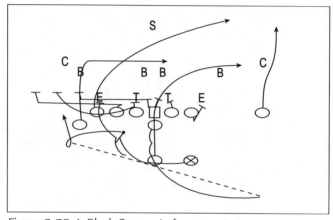

Figure 3-35. L Black Screen Left versus 4-4

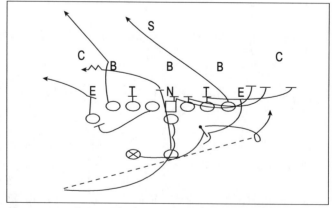

Figure 3-36. Lance Black Screen Right versus 5-3

4

Blue Series

The Blue series is a belly lead series to the halfback-aligned side, with the fullback carrying the ball. The word belly tells the quarterback to reverse pivot and the fullback to arc into his assigned hole. The halfback lead blocks the first linebacker to threaten. Features of this series include the frequent use of wingback motion to either block out on the defensive end, lead on an outside linebacker, release for a pass, or become the ballcarrier on a counter or tackle trap towards the side he originally aligned. This series is an adaptation of the wing-T 80 series.

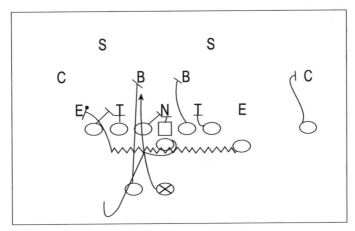

Figure 4-1. Blue series versus 5-2 (Ram)

Counters, tackle traps, and play-action passes are used to offset defenses that squeeze toward the base plays in the series with slants to motion, stunts to motion, and secondary rotation to motion. The formations of choice are Ram/Lion for power and supplemental play-action passes. R/L formations are used to balance the run with the pass. R/L formations provide less power, but a more extensive pass package.

For simplicity of presentation, only plays from Ram and L formations will be diagramed. However, the diagramed plays are run from both Ram and Lion and from both R and L.

33/34 Blast

The base running play from Ram/Lion versus the 4-4 and 4-3 is Kick Blue 33/34 Blast.

Line—Blast tells the linemen to double-team the first down lineman inside the hole called. For 33/34 Blast, the tackle and guard will double-team the tackle. If, however, the defensive lineman is inside of the guard, the guard will audible to off and the double-team is now done with the guard and center. The tackle would then drive block the first inside linebacker. The center and backside guard scoop playside to prevent the inside linebackers from running through the A gaps.

Halfback—Leads through the hole and blocks the first linebacker in the hole to the inside.

Flex end—Bluffs a down block on the defensive end by placing his hands on the defensive end's outside shoulder, then drive blocks the outside linebacker.

Wing—Motions across (kick motion) and trap blocks out on the defensive end. A well-coached defensive end will first start to fight the flex end's down block. This practice will delay his move across the line of scrimmage and to the inside and makes the wing's kick-out block easier.

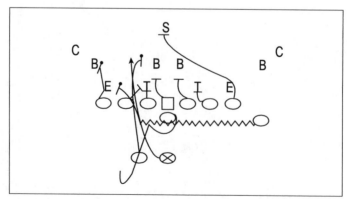

Figure 4-2. Ram Kick Blue 33 Blast versus 4-4

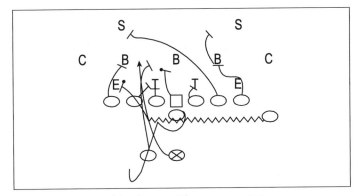

Figure 4-3. Ram Kick Blue 33 Blast versus 4-3

31/32 Blast

The base running play from Ram/Lion versus the 5-2 and 5-3 is Kick Blue 31/32 Blast. Versus the 5-2, the flex end can double-team the defensive tackle if the tackle needs help, but he usually blocks the outside linebacker versus 5-3 or the safety versus 5-2. The first defensive lineman inside the hole is the nose, and the center and playside guard double-team him.

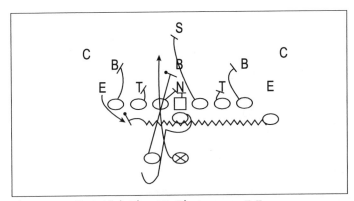

Figure 4-4. Ram Kick Blue 31 Blast versus 5-3

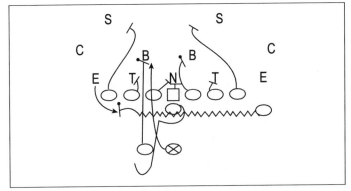

Figure 4-5. Ram Kick Blue 31 Blast versus 5-2

35/36 Blast

Versus 5-3 and 5-2, the flex end and tackle will double-team the tackle and the motioning wing will kick out the end. Versus the 4-4 and 4-3, this play should only be called if the defensive end aligns inside the flex end or slants inside to negate the wing's kick-out block. The snap count for crack is two.

Playside guard—Base blocks the tackle.

Flex end—Double-teams the defensive end with the tackle.

Wing—Crack motions across and leads on the outside linebacker or cornerback.

Halfback—Leads outside the double-team and blocks the first inside linebacker to threaten.

Fullback—Bellys at the tackle's back until the handoff is secure and then veers outside the double-team block.

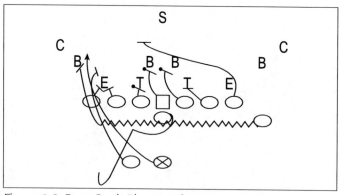

Figure 4-6. Ram Crack Blue 35 Blast versus 4-4

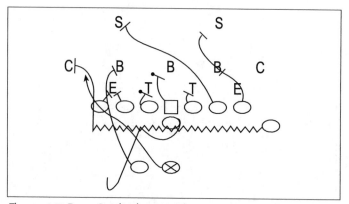

Figure 4-7. Ram Crack Blue 35 Blast versus 4-3

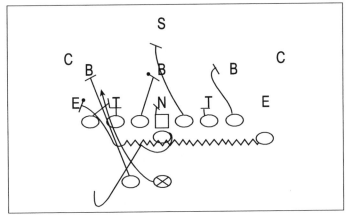

Figure 4-8. Ram Kick Blue 35 Blast versus 5-3

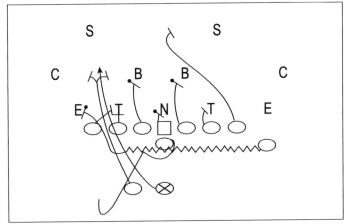

Figure 4-9. Ram Kick Blue 35 Blast versus 5-2

Base Running Plays from R/L Blue

A good Blue variation is to run crack motion to the split end side.

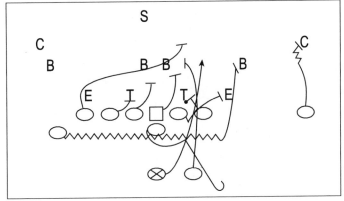

Figure 4-10. L Crack Blue 34X versus 4-4

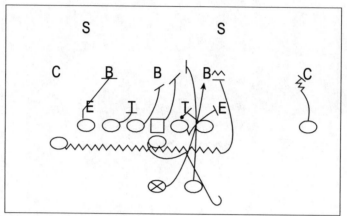

Figure 4-11. L Crack Blue 34X versus 4-3

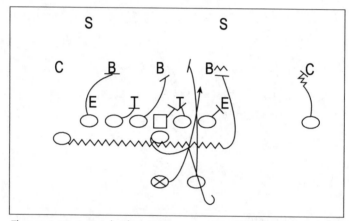

Figure 4-12. L Crack Blue 34X versus 4-3 (Note: if the defense reduces to the split end side, the X block is off and center and playside guard double-team the A gap defensive tackle.)

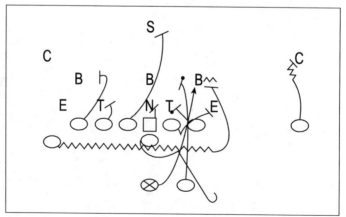

Figure 4-13. L Crack Blue 34X versus 5-3

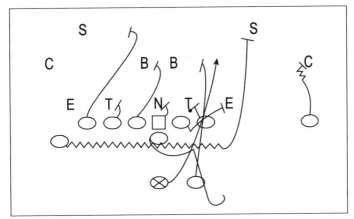

Figure 4-14. L Crack Blue 34X versus 5-2

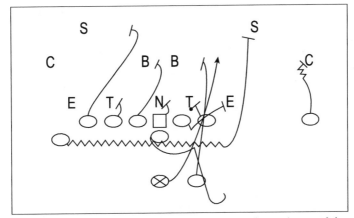

Figure 4-15. L Crack Blue 34X versus 5-2 and 5-3 (Note: If the defense doesn't reduce, X is off and blast is on.)

Tips on X blocking: the playside tackle fires out and aims at his guard's down hand. This angle gives him enough lead that he should be able to drive his head across the front of the defensive tackle. The guard steps back 18 inches with his outside foot and makes it the weight bearing pivot foot as he swings his inside foot directly at the end. Simultaneously, he picks up speed and adjusts his direction to trap out on the defensive end. It is important that he stays relatively low to deliver an effective kick out block.

31/32 Fan

Blue 31/32 Fan is a subtle misdirection play run only versus the 4-4. Running it from a double tight end formation insures that one of the defensive tackles won't be reduced.

Fullback—Initially heads for the 3/4 hole and keeps curving back to the middle.

Quarterback—Spins in place to avoid forcing the fullback wide.

Wing—His motion creates the appearance of a wide play to the linebackers.

Halfback—Aligns his heels even with the fullback's toes and is slightly tighter in width. He always blocks the playside linebacker, while the center blocks the awayside linebacker.

The angle for blocks on the rest of the defense are excellent. This play from Sword/Lance is also shown (Figure 4-17) and is identical, except no motion is involved.

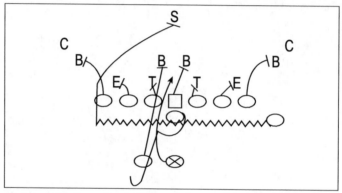

Figure 4-16. Ram Crack Blue 31 Fan versus 4-4

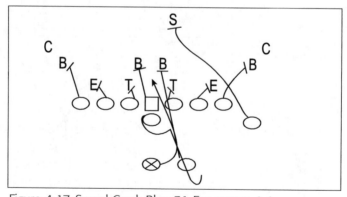

Figure 4-17. Sword Crack Blue 31 Fan versus 4-4

45/46 Counter

The counter should be taught first from a strong set. And, then evolve to motioning the wing to one side and countering back to the side he originally aligned on. This counter is excellent because both the halfback and fullback fake away from the play hole. Thus, it is difficult for the linebackers to find the wingback, and they also are often walled off from the play hole. The wing must cross in front of the halfback. The halfback also adjusts his speed and arcs out initially to allow the wing to cross in front.

Stopping inside penetration is a must in order to have a good counter game. Versus the 4-4, the playside guard, who double-team blocks on the defensive tackle, should see the linebacker over him and come off the double if the linebacker tries to run through his A gap. Likewise, the playside guard versus the 5-3 is responsible for the middle linebacker, but combos to him, helping the center with the noseman first. The fullback and halfback directional fakes should delay the middle linebacker long enough for the guard to combo the noseman and still cut off the middle linebacker. The fullback fakes through the backside guard's initial spot and will block the middle linebacker if he stunts through that area.

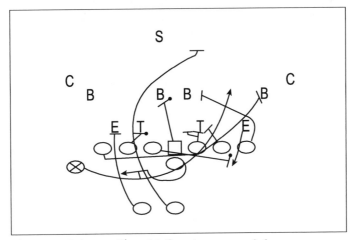

Figure 4-18. Lance Blue 46 Counter versus 4-4

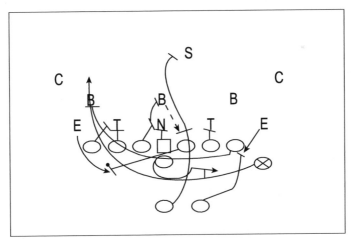

Figure 4-19. Sword Blue 45 Counter versus 5-3

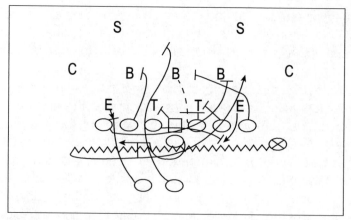

Figure 4-20. Ram Crack Blue 46 Counter versus 4-3 (Note: the center blocks back on the defensive tackle, the tight end down blocks on the middle linebacker, and the flex end leads through the hole and blocks the outside linebacker. The ball is snapped when the wing is in front of the halfback. The wing takes two more steps outside, pivots back away from the line, and comes behind the fullback's 33/34 fake.)

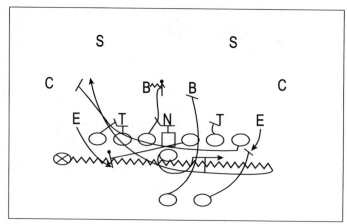

Figure 4-21. Lion Crack Blue 45 Counter versus 5-2

41/42 Tackle Trap

Like the counter, the best teaching approach is to first learn the play thoroughly from a strong set. Evolve to motioning the wing to the opposite side and then bring him back up the middle on the tackle trap. The quarterback gives an inside handoff to the wing. Backfield timing is identical to counter.

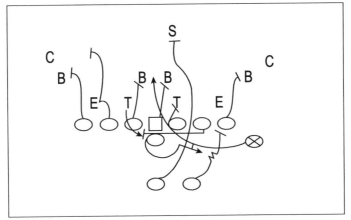

Figure 4-22. Sword Blue 41 Tackle Trap versus 4-4 (Note: versus the 4-4, the playside tackle shoves the defensive end out, then walls off the center area.)

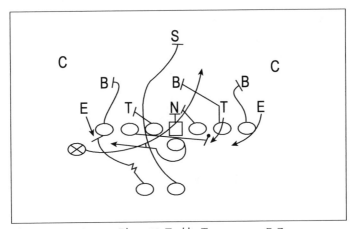

Figure 4-23. Lance Blue 42 Tackle Trap versus 5-3

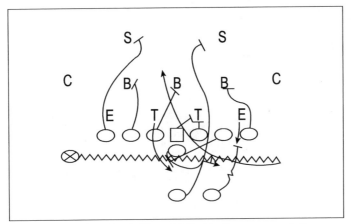

Figure 4-24. Lion Crack Blue 44 Tackle Trap versus 4-3

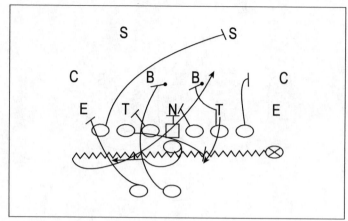

Figure 4-25. Ram Crack Blue 42 Tackle Trap versus 5-2

The Tackle Trap can also be run successfully from R/L, which gives that formation a needed counter in the Blue series.

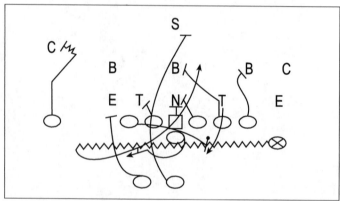

Figure 4-26. R Crack Blue 42 Tackle Trap versus 5-3

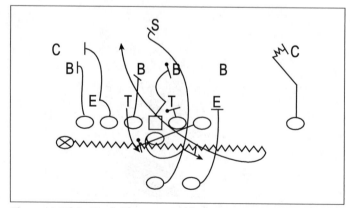

Figure 4-27. L Crack Blue 41 Tackle Trap versus 4-4

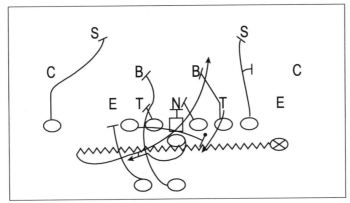

Figure 4-28. R Crack Blue 42 Tackle Trap versus 5-2

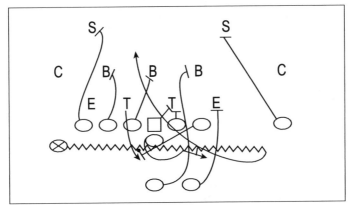

Figure 4-29. L Crack Blue 41 Tackle Trap versus 4-3

Blue Pass

Two types of Blue passes exist: Ram/Lion passes with the flex end aligned as a tight end and R/L with the flex end split. For both, the pass blocking is turn-back protection. The fullback fakes a 33/34 and then widens to block the C gap. The halfback aims for the flex end's spot and is in a position to double-team with the fullback or, if a stunt is on, pick up the outside rusher.

Line—Uses turn-back blocking.

Flex end—Slows to show a block on the outside linebacker, then sprints to the corner.

Wing—Runs a seven-yard corner out.

Tight end—Runs an across at 10 yards and is a safety valve if the flex end and wing are covered. A safety rotating to help his cornerback and outside linebacker will leave the tight end open.

Quarterback—Reads both #1s simultaneously and throws to the most open receiver. If neither is open, looks to the tight end who has a good chance of being open.

For the balance of this book, to reduce the volume of diagrams, each type of pass play will be shown versus an even and odd front for pass blocking and a three and two-deep secondary to throw against.

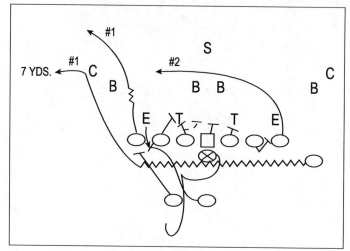

Figure 4-30. Ram Crack Blue Pass Left versus 4-4

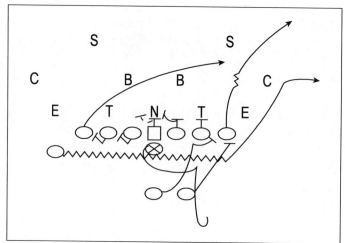

Figure 4-31. Lion Crack Blue Pass Right versus 5-2 (Note: pass routes are identical versus both three deep and two deep.)

Blue Pass Flood

Standard Blue pass turn-back protection is used. Versus the 4-4, the flex end chips the defensive end on his way to a 20-yard deep corner route. This route will slow his pass rush. The halfback chips the defensive end with his hands to help the fullback block the defensive end, then slants outside to five yards depth. The wing runs a 12-yard out. The flex end's route clears out. The quarterback will read both the wing and halfback simultaneously to throw to the open man.

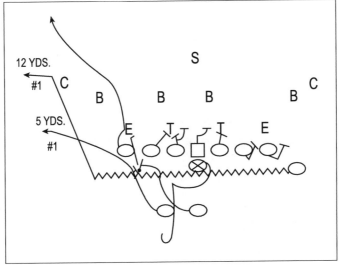

Figure 4-32. Ram Crack Blue Pass Left Flood versus 4-4

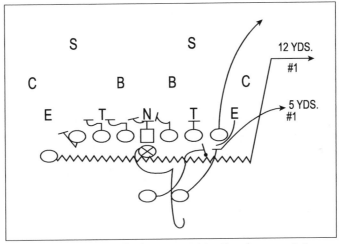

Figure 4-33. Lion Crack Blue Pass Right Flood versus 5-2

R/L Blue Pass

This pass features the flex end plus decoys the defense, allowing the other receivers to get open.

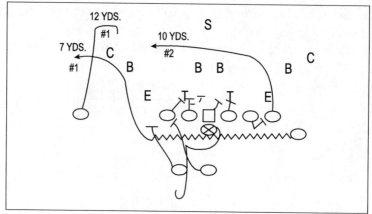

Figure 4-34. R Crack Blue Pass Left versus 4-4 (Note: this base pass has the flex end hooking in at 12 yards back to 10 yards and is a high percentage completion play.)

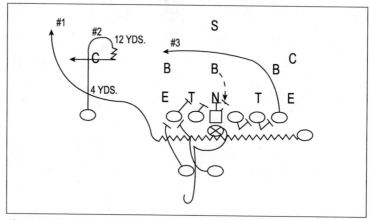

Figure 4-35. R Crack Blue Pass Left-4 Wheel versus 5-3 (Note: the wing's wheel route is primary. The flex end hooks 12 yards back to 10, hesitates, then whips out as a #2 receiver.)

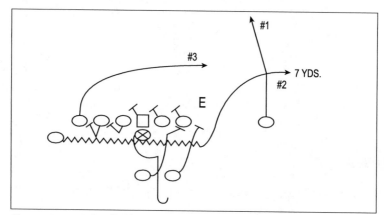

Figure 4-36. L Crack Blue Pass Right Skinny Post

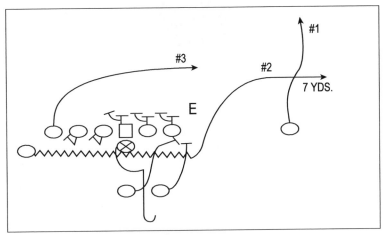

Figure 4-37. L Crack Blue Pass Right-Fade

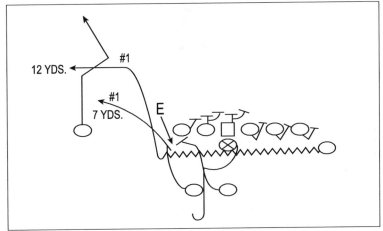

Figure 4-38. R Crack Blue Pass Left-Flood (Note: the quarterback reads the wing and halfback and hits the open man.)

5

Green Series

The Green series is a small group of wing-T 80 series plays called 80 down. It is a simple five-play series with two base plays (fullback belly and option), one misdirection play (counter), and two passes (Green pass and Green throwback). Ram/Lion and R/L formations can be mixed so no discernable pattern exists; yet, the best formation can be used for the play called.

The angle blocking, the wing blocking on the second level, the option threat, and the misdirection threat all fit together to make these plays solid run plays. The halfback learns to anticipate the actual snap and uses a one-step motion to be almost behind the fullback at the snap.

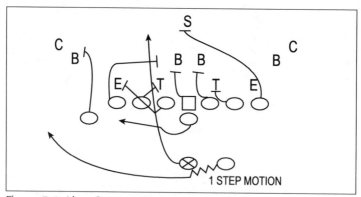

Figure 5-1. Lion Green 33X versus 4-4

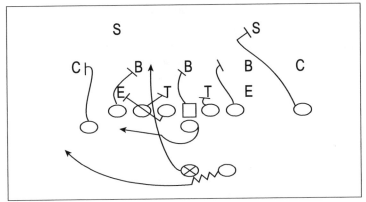

Figure 5-2. L Green 33X versus 4-3

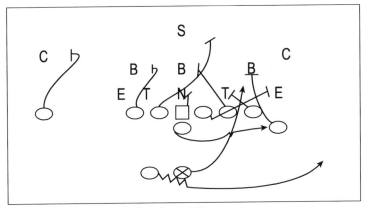

Figure 5-3. R Green 36G versus 5-3

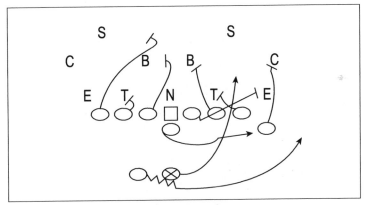

Figure 5-4. Ram Green 36G versus 5-2

Green Option

The defensive front and how hard the defensive perimeter players are to block will determine who to option. Versus the 4-4 or 4-3, the tight end will block the defensive end, and the usual choice is to option the outside linebacker. The wing will release and block the cornerback. Versus the 5-2, when the defensive end attacks the tight end's outside shoulder, the wing will block the defensive end and the quarterback will option the cornerback. Versus the 5-3, the tight end will block the outside linebacker and the quarterback will option the end. To clarify who to option, add B (outside linebacker), C (cornerback), or E (end), to the play call.

Fullback—Arcs toward the tackle and carries out the fake. Blocks the linebacker if the guard or tackle need help; otherwise, blocks the safety.

Playside guard and tackle—Will swing block versus the 4-4, because the combo block is usually too slow to block the linebacker on options.

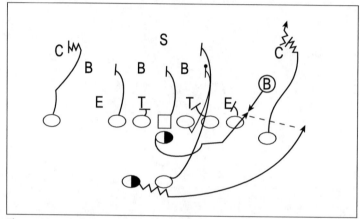

Figure 5-5. R Green Option Right-B versus 4-4

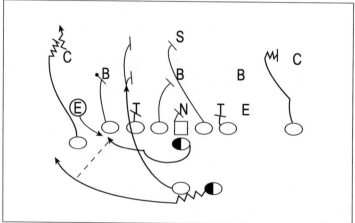

Figure 5-6. L Green Option Left-E versus 5-3

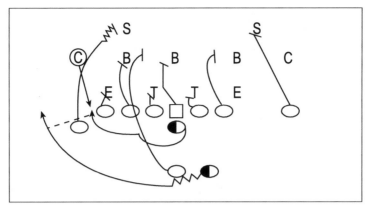

Figure 5-7. L Green Option Left-C versus 4-3

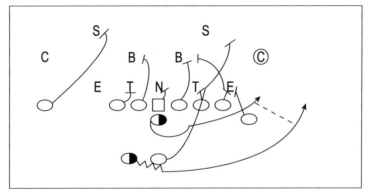

Figure 5-8. R Green Option Right-C versus 5-2

Green 45/46 Counter

The blocking for Green 45/46 Counter is identical to all the counters run in the multiple offense system, but the backfield action is different. Also, like all counters, the quarterback makes an outside handoff.

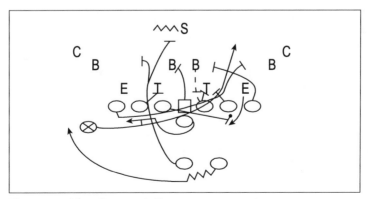

Figure 5-9. Lion Green 46 Counter versus 4-4

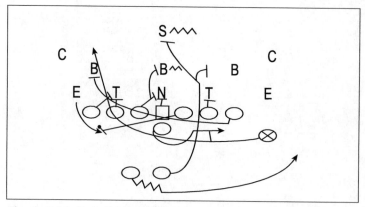

Figure 5-10. Ram Green 45 Counter versus 5-3 (Note: versus the 5-3 and 5-2, the playside guard combos with the center on the nose guard to the linebacker.)

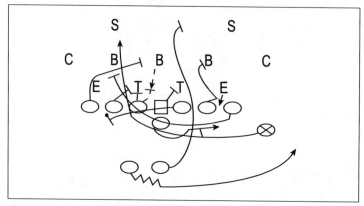

Figure 5-11. Ram Green 45 Counter versus 4-3 (Note: the backside tackle chip blocks the defensive end to prevent him from disrupting the handoff.)

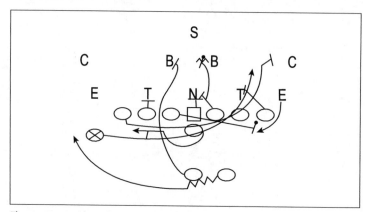

Figure 5-12. Lion Green 46 Counter versus 5-2

Green Pass

Turn-back pass blocking makes the protection versus odd and even fronts essentially the same. The quarterback reads the tight end and wing simultaneously and throws to the open receiver. If neither one is open, the quarterback should read the backside end.

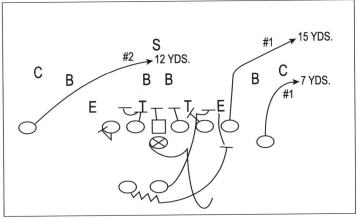

Figure 5-13. R Green Pass Right versus 4-4

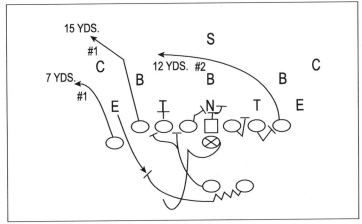

Figure 5-14. Lion Green Pass Left versus 5-3

Green Throwback

Turn-back blocking is also used with Green throwback pass. The quarterback drops deeper than on the Green pass and reads the tight end drag route, then the split end fade in route, and then the wing.

The wing splits the two deep. If three deep, the wing hooks up three yards behind the safety's original spot. Thus, if the safety slides to cover the flex end's in route, the wing will be open.

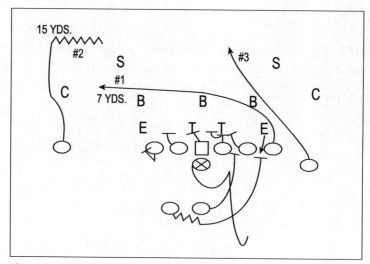

Figure 5-15. R Green Throwback versus 4-3

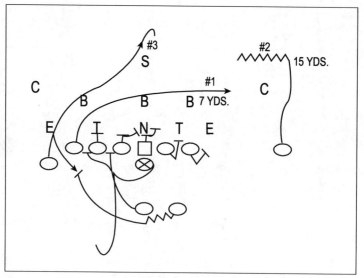

Figure 5-16. L Green Throwback versus 5-3

6

Red Series

The Red series features quick dives to the fullback and halfback, deceptive plays by faking dives and running elsewhere, or passing. This series originates from the split-T inside belly series. It serves as a change-up in style from the rest of the offense. Its simplicity and quickness may surprise defenses geared to slow up the Black and Blue series. If the offense has two running backs that are quick off the ball and are hard to tackle, the Red series can become one of the main series.

The Quarterback in the Red Series

The quarterback opens at a 90-degree angle to the side of the play call and hands off for a quick dive or fakes the dive and moves slightly back to mesh with the trailing halfback who is sprinting towards the off-tackle (5/6) hole. The quarterback will either handoff to the trailing halfback, keep and follow him through the 5/6 hole, or keep and run wide. If the option is called, the quarterback will fake the dive, then attack the off-tackle area with a double option keep or pitch to the trailing back. Red 45/46 Counter comes off of the option fake. The quarterback makes an outside handoff to the wing after faking the dive.

The coach should select the perimeter plays that best fit the quarterback's abilities. The first decision is whether to run the option and a keep or just one of those two. Then, if keep is the desired play, decide whether to run both the 5/6 hole belly follow and the 7/8 hole belly keep or just one of the two. With a fast quarterback, the option and the 7/8 hole keep are a good selection. The logic is that when the quarterback keeps on the option he'll duck up through the 5/6 hole. And, the 7/8 hole keep allows him to hit the wide holes. With a quarterback with average speed, the 5/6 hole belly follow is probably the best selection.

When the defense squeezes down to stop the 3 and 4 hole dives or the Blue 3 and 4 hole blasts, they will be vulnerable to the off-tackle plays. Thus, the wide dive 25/26 is a good selection.

33/34 Dive

Refer to Figures 6-1 through 6-5.

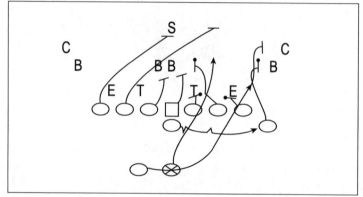

Figure 6-1. Ram Red 34 Dive versus 4-4 (Note: the tight end drives his head inside the defensive end to stop penetration. The playside guard and tackle combo the tackle with the tackle coming off to help the center seal off the inside linebacker.)

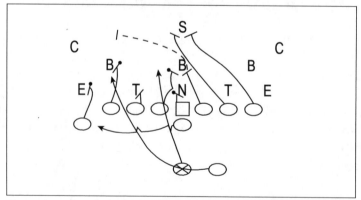

Figure 6-2. Lion Red 33 Dive versus 5-3 (Note: the playside guard and center combo the nose with the guard coming off to block the inside linebacker.)

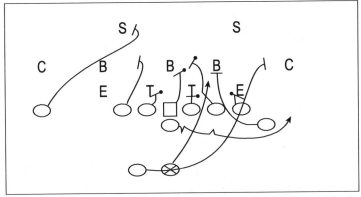

Figure 6-3. R Red 34 Dive versus 4-3 (Note: Wings "duck" block, i.e., duck under the tight end.)

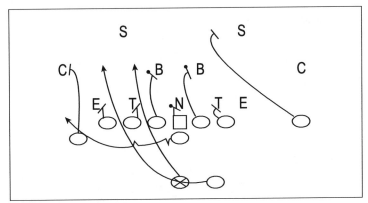

Figure 6-4. L Red 33 Dive versus 5-2

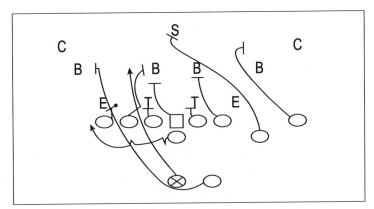

Figure 6-5. Rex Red 33 Dive versus 4-4

23/24 Dive

Refer to Figures 6-6 through 6-9.

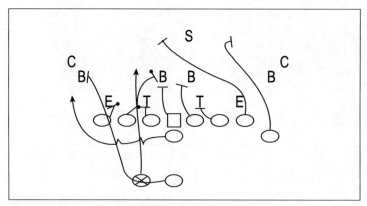

Figure 6-6. Ram Red 23 Dive versus 4-4

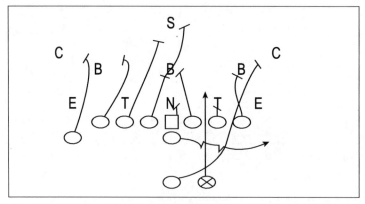

Figure 6-7. Lion Red 24 Dive versus 5-3

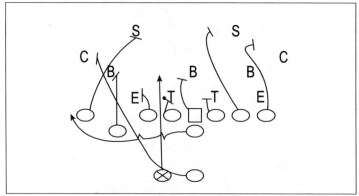

Figure 6-8. Lou Red 23 Dive versus 4-3

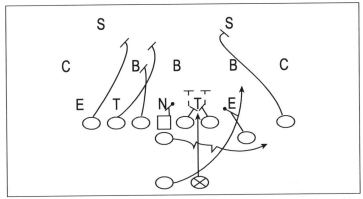

Figure 6-9. Rex Red 24 Dive versus 5-2 (Note: the playside tackle and guard combo the reduced defensive tackle and linebacker by attempting to drive the tackle backward into the backer. If the tackle works inside or outside, the freed-up lineman will come off onto the linebacker.)

25/26 Wide Dive

Use kick and crack motion when running Red 25/26 Wide Dive from Ram/Lion.

Halfback—Aims at the tackle's back and then veers out.

Flex end—Blocks down on the defensive end aligned on his inside shoulder. If the defensive end is head-up or on the outside shoulder of the flex end, he will block the outside linebacker and the wing will block out on the defensive end.

Quarterback—Sprints to the handoff point, then fakes the option.

Fullback—Fakes the option.

Playside guard and tackle—Swing blocks versus the 4-4's defensive tackle and linebacker.

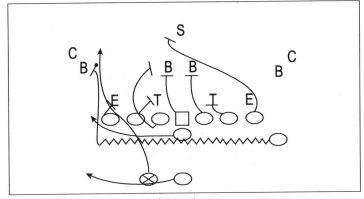

Figure 6-10. Ram Crack Red 25 Dive versus 4-4

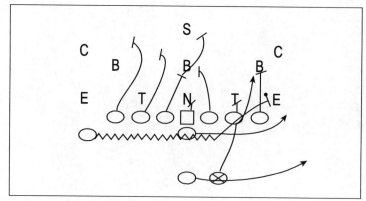

Figure 6-11. Lion Kick Red 26 Dive versus 5-3

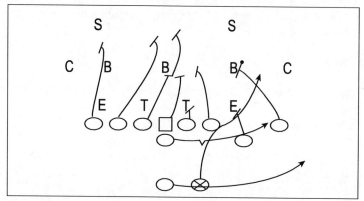

Figure 6-12. Rex Red 26 Dive versus 4-3 (Note: the slot blocks the defensive end the easiest way, and the flex end blocks inside on the first threat off the line of scrimmage.)

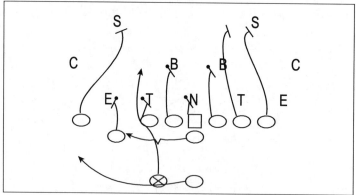

Figure 6-13. Lou Red 25 Dive versus 5-2

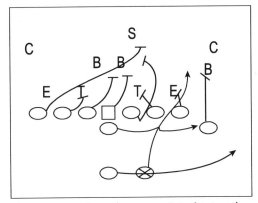

Figure 6-14. Sword versus 4-4 (Note: the tight end blocks the defensive end, and the wing blocks the first threat off the line of scrimmage.)

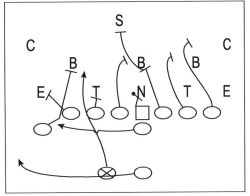

Figure 6-15. Lance versus 5-3 (Note: the tight end blocks the defensive end, and the wing ducks under and blocks the first threat off the line of scrimmage.)

25/26 Belly

Halfback—Aims for the fullback's aligned toes and curves to the 5/6 hole.

Quarterback—Makes a good fake to the fullback, angles back to the handoff, and then fakes a 17/18 keep.

Tight end—Blocks the defensive end the easiest way.

Wing—Blocks the outside linebacker. The wing may have to duck under the tight end as shown versus the 5-3.

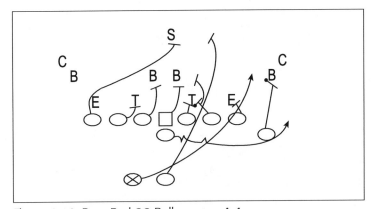

Figure 6-16. Ram Red 26 Belly versus 4-4

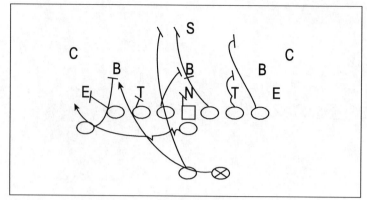

Figure 6-17. Lion Red 25 Belly versus 5-3

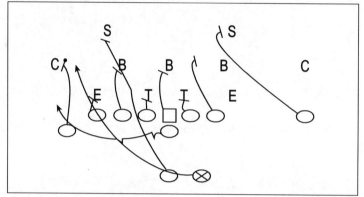

Figure 6-18. L Red 25 Belly versus 4-3

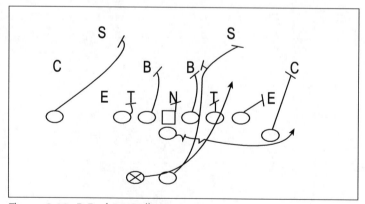

Figure 6-19. R Red 26 Belly versus 5-2

35/36 Belly

Refer to Figures 6-20 through 6-23.

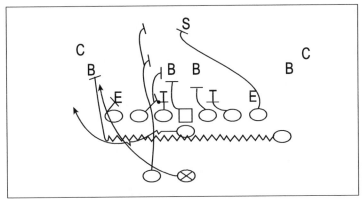

Figure 6-20. Ram Crack Red 25 Belly versus 4-4

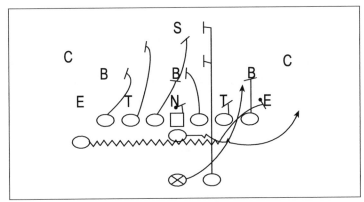

Figure 6-21. Lion Kick Red 26 Belly versus 5-3

From the strong sets (Sword/Lance and Rex/Lou), use the same blocking as for Red 25/26 Wide Dive from Rex/Lou and Sword/Lance.

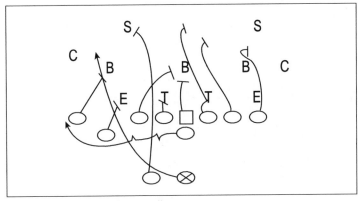

Figure 6-22. Lou Red 35 Belly versus 4-3

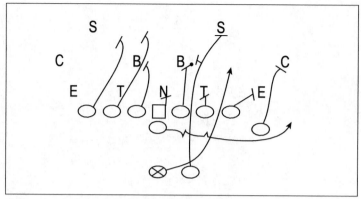

Figure 6-23. Sword Red 36 Belly versus 5-2

5/6 Hole Follow

Follow is always run off a belly fake to the same side, with the back faking the belly becoming a lead blocker. It is always a 5/6 hole play. Follow is an ideal play for a physical quarterback who may lack the speed for running outside.

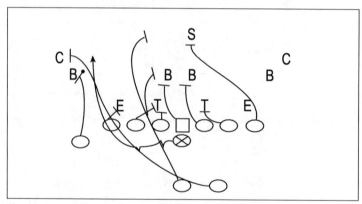

Figure 6-24. Lion Red 25 Follow versus 4-4

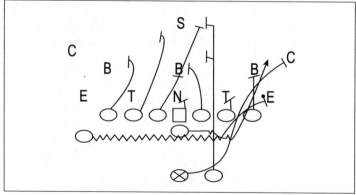

Figure 6-25. Lion Kick Red 36 Follow versus 5-3

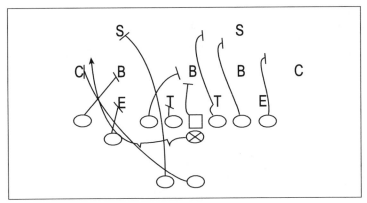

Figure 6-26. Lou Red 35 Follow versus 4-3

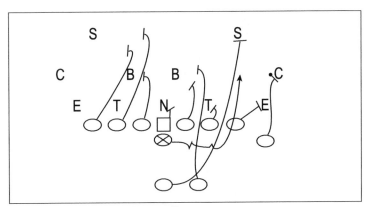

Figure 6-27. Sword Red 36 Follow versus 5-2

7/8 Hole Keep

17/18 belly keep is an ideal play for the quarterback who has good outside speed.

Fullback/Halfback—It is important to run the 5/6 belly route and not widen to get the cornerback until through the hole.

Quarterback—Runs around the block on the contain man (outside linebacker and defensive end versus the 4-4 and 4-3, defensive end versus the 5-3 and 5-2). Then, runs at the cornerback to freeze him and aid the fullback's block on him. Be prepared to run inside or outside the cornerback, depending on the block on him.

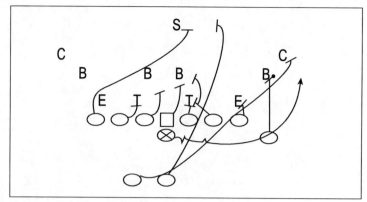

Figure 6-28. Ram Red 18 Belly Keep versus 4-4

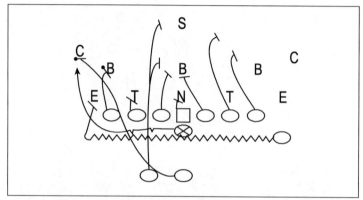

Figure 6-29. Ram Crack Red 17 Belly Keep versus 5-3 (Note: the wing motions wide and crack blocks the defensive end.)

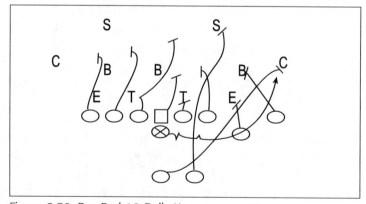

Figure 6-30. Rex Red 18 Belly Keep versus 4-3

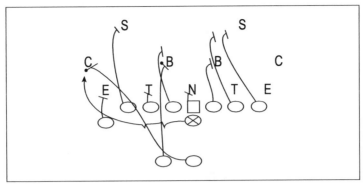

Figure 6-31. Lance Red 17 Belly Keep versus 5-2

Option RT/LT

To run this play, the fullback should be able to run sideways with quickness and catch the pitch. To make Red Option unpredictable, fake dive to either back and run the option with either back. The hardest man to block on the perimeter is designated as the man to option. The wing or flex end will run off the corner rather than stalk block him.

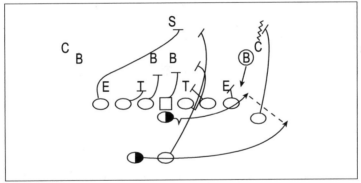

Figure 6-32. Ram Red Option Right-B versus 4-4 (Note: the halfback can use one-step motion to get into the proper pitch relationship.)

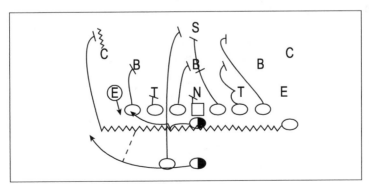

Figure 6-33. Ram Crack Red Option Left-E versus 5-3

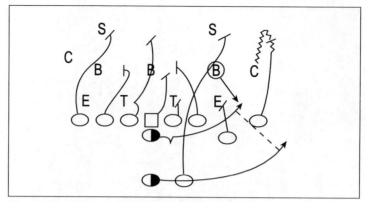

Figure 6-34. Rex Red Option Right-B versus 4-3

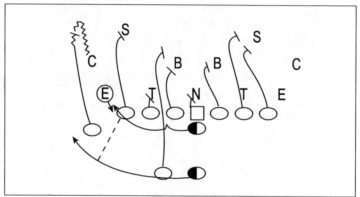

Figure 6-35. Lance Red Option Left-E versus 5-2

45/46 Counter

The blocking for Red 45/46 Counter is identical to Blue, Black, and Green counters.

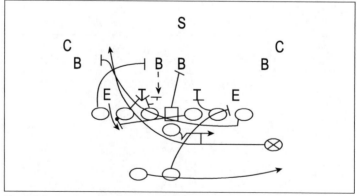

Figure 6-36. Ram Red 45 Counter versus 4-4

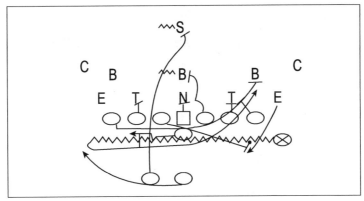

Figure 6-37. Ram Crack Red 46 Counter versus 5-3

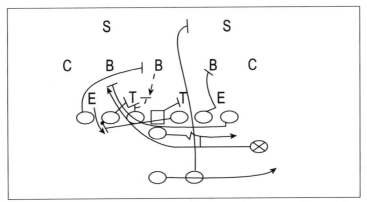

Figure 6-38. Sword Red 45 Counter versus 4-3 (Note: the backside tackle chip blocks the defensive end to prevent a disruption in the handoff.)

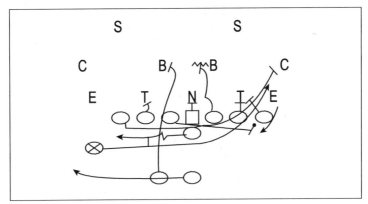

Figure 6-39. Lance Red 46 Counter versus 5-2

Banana Pass

Flex end and tight end—Start out at 45 degrees and curve back over their original alignment at 10 yards.

Slot—Versus a three deep, hooks at approximately eight yards and splits the distance between the linebacker depth and the safety. The goal is to hold the safety in center field and split the inside linebacker's zone drops. Versus man coverage or two deep, slants deep through the middle.

Quarterback—Takes two steps toward the dive back, gives a handoff fake, then takes two more steps back. Rapidly reads all three receivers and throws to the open man. Alternately, the quarterback could take his two steps and fake, then turn on that spot, read the receivers, and throw.

Line—Turn-back block protection is used.

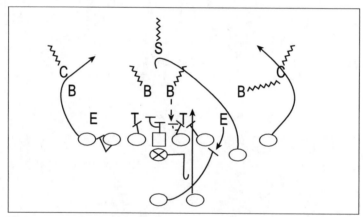

Figure 6-40. Rex Red Banana versus 4-4 three deep

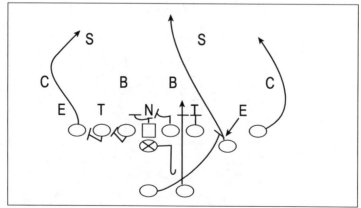

Figure 6-41. Rex Red Banana versus 5-2 two deep

Belly Pass

Tight end—Runs drag route at 10 yards. Versus the 5-2, blocks the defensive end.

Wing—Motions across and runs a corner route.

Flex end—Blocks the defensive end for two counts, then slants out at a five-yard depth.

Halfback—Fakes the dive, then follows the wing to the corner.

Quarterback—Fakes the dive, angles deep on the belly fake, and then keeps coming back and out while searching for an open receiver. Tucks and runs if no open receivers.

Fullback—Hooks the defensive end by blocking with the head to the outside and swinging the feet around.

Line—Turn-back block protection is used.

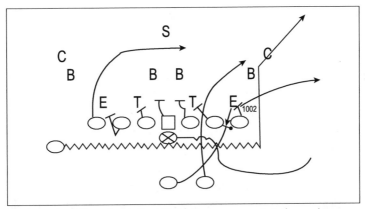

Figure 6-42. Lion Crack Red Belly Pass versus 4-4 three deep

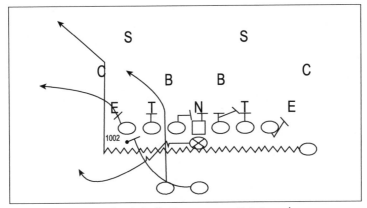

Figure 6-43. Ram Crack Belly Pass versus 5-2 two deep

7

Orange Series

The Orange series is based on the wing-T 30 series, which features the fullback leading the halfback. However, a significant difference exists. Orange plays go weakside or away from the wing, while the wing-T 30 series' lead and power plays go towards the wing. Because a lot of wing-T plays are run to the strongside, the weakside Orange series breaks this tendency. This series is very simple. Versus an even front (4-3 and 4-4), run 23/24X or 23/24 Blast if the defensive alignment makes a cross block difficult. Versus an odd front (5-2 and 5-3), the 21/22 Blast and 25/26 Power are good play calls. Bootleg and boot passes can also be run from these play fakes.

Fullback—Leads weak through the A, B, or C gap based on the play call.

Halfback—Follows the fullback and either takes the handoff from the quarterback or fakes.

Quarterback—Reverse pivots and turns his back to the defense while handing off or faking it. Then, runs the boot pass-action on all plays. Shows pass even when keeping on the bootleg.

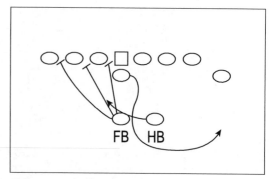

Figure 7-1. Basic Orange series backfield action from Sword formation

23/24X versus 4-3 and 4-4

If, at the line of scrimmage, the playside defensive tackle aligns in the A gap, thus too far inside for the tackle to down block him, the guard will call, "Off." This call will cancel the cross block and automatically creates a double-team by the playside guard and center. The playside tackle will then block the first man on the line outside the double-team.

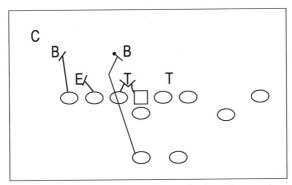

Figure 7-2. Rex Orange 23X called. Left guard at line of scrimmage calls, "Off."

This play is excellent to coach a planned downfield cutback, because either the slot in Rex/Lou versus a three deep secondary or the backside tackle in Sword/Lance versus a two deep secondary are assigned to block the safety. The fullback has a tough block, because either the playside inside linebacker or the middle linebacker scraping is a difficult target to block. The center's job is to prevent a linebacker run through the A gap. If the center cannot block the linebacker, he looks for the backside linebacker flowing toward the play.

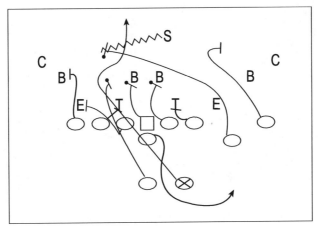

Figure 7-3. Rex Orange 23X versus 4-4

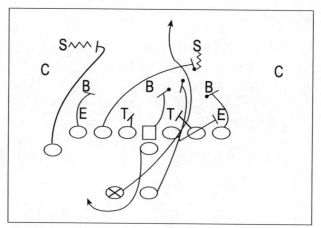

Figure 7-4. Lance Orange 24X versus 4-3

21/22 Blast

Versus odd defenses, the inside blast is the base Orange play. Just like 23/24X, this play is a planned cutback. Aligning the halfback in the guard-tackle gap on the strongside creates lateral defensive pursuit as the backs flow to the weakside, more so than if the backfield is lined up in an I formation and ran the same play. The quarterback should swing his offside foot directly at the halfback's aligned position and angle back to make the handoff to avoid forcing the halfback too wide. The halfback's ideal route is a slight curve to the playside guard's inside foot.

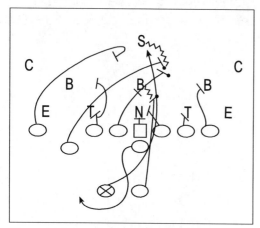

Figure 7-5. Lou Orange 22 Blast versus 5-3

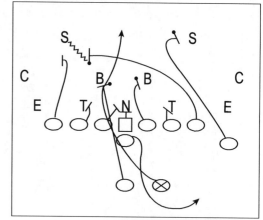

Figure 7-6. Sword Orange 21 Blast versus 5-2

If the defense overshifts toward the strength of the formation, the blast double-team moves over one position.

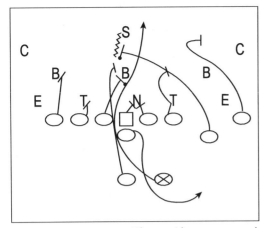

Figure 7-7. Rex 21 Blast with center and backside guard double-team on an overshifted nose versus 5-3

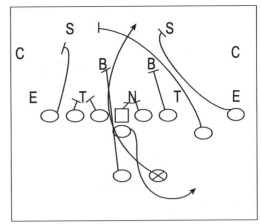

Figure 7-8. Rex 21 Blast with center and backside guard double-team on nose, and playside guard and tackle double-team on the tackle versus overshifted 5-2

21/22 Fan

This play is good to occasionally run against the 4-4, particularly if the center and fullback can each get good position and decent blocks on the inside linebackers. The fullback blocks the holeside linebacker, and the center blocks away. Fan out angles are created on all defenders. Wider line spacing is suggested on this play.

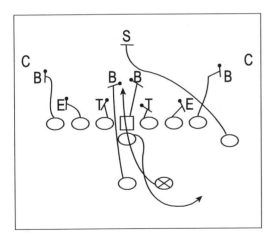

Figure 7-9. Rex Orange 21 Fan versus 4-4

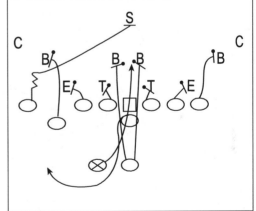

Figure 7-10. Lou Orange 22 Fan versus 4-4

25/26 Power versus the 5-2 and 5-3

This powerful and relatively fast hitting off-tackle play has good angles versus defenses with contain ends. A combo block by the tackle and tight end to the inside linebacker will wall off the linebacker and create a good run alley for the halfback.

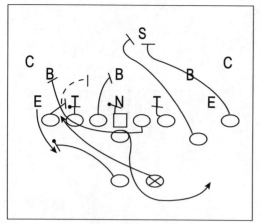

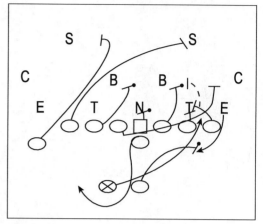

Figure 7-11. Rex Orange 25 Power versus 5-3

Figure 7-12. Lance Orange 26 Power versus 5-2

Orange Bootleg RT/LT

A good running quarterback is necessary for this play to be successful. The quarterback hides the ball on his backside hip initially and then holds the ball in pass position, while running wide and looking at the backside tight end. The backside tight end runs a decoy slant route through the safety area to get the secondary to hesitate and consider pass, thus slowing up their pursuit. Versus the 5-3 and 5-2, the playside guard checks the wing's block on the defensive end before leading downfield.

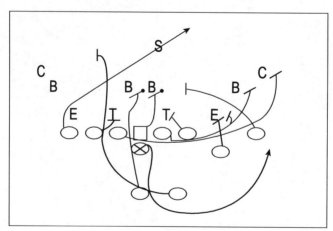

Figure 7-13. Rex Orange Bootleg Right versus 4-4

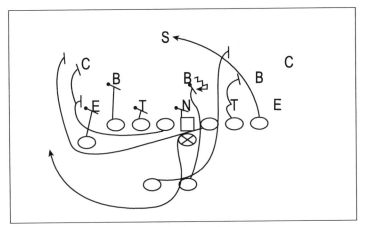

Figure 7-14. Lance Orange Bootleg Left versus 5-3

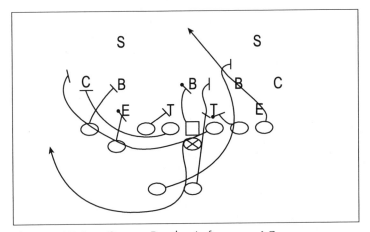

Figure 7-15. Lou Orange Bootleg Left versus 4-3

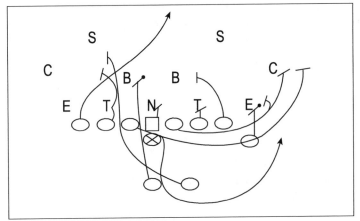

Figure 7-16. Sword Orange Bootleg Right versus 5-2

Orange Boot Pass

The pass routes are identical to Black Boot from a strong set (Sword/Lance in Figures 3-31 through 3-34 in Chapter 3), except Orange Boot has one less receiver and requires the backside flex end to run a 12-yard deep across route versus all defenses.

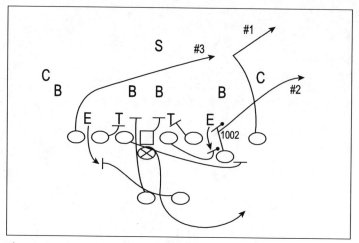

Figure 7-17. Rex Orange Boot Right versus 4-4

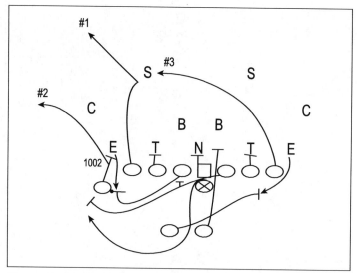

Figure 7-18. Lance Orange Boot Left (Note: Backside guard versus 5-2 must check playside guards for a linebacker blitz before pulling wide.)

Orange Pass RT/LT

This play is a good alternative to the boot pass when the quarterback has problems getting outside the contain rush and for the inside linebacker's blitz through the playside A gap. This play keeps the playside guard in to block the A gap, and the quarterback drops back after faking to the halfback. The misdirection effect still occurs with the 25/26 Power Fake Away, plus the quarterback has greater passing accuracy from the play-action dropback. The fullback fills for the backside pulling guard, and the halfback blocks the backside defensive end. The flat route receiver blocks for two counts before releasing into the route.

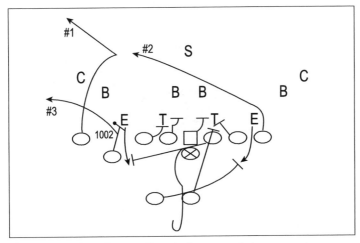

Figure 7-19. Lou Orange Pass Left versus 4-4

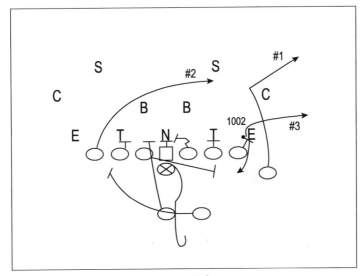

Figure 7-20. Sword Orange Pass Right versus 5-2

8

White Series

The White series is a quick pitch series. It only has three to five plays, but all have big play potential. Essentially developed by the NFL in the early 1950s, it is by far the quickest way to run outside.

White Pitch

The pitch can be run from three different formations:
- Toward the strongside
- Toward the weakside
- Toward the weakside with motion from the strongside

By alignment and movement, the defense will dictate what formation is best. The offense should practice all three each week, and then decide what formations to use in a game after looking at the opponent's defense.

Halfback—Arcs back slightly, catches the pitch, and stays with the convoy of tackle and guard until the tackle blocks. He then uses the guard as his lead. Gets all the easy yards possible while going wide and then looks for a cutback.

Playside tackle—Pulls and deepens to get around the blocks of the slot/wing and the ends. Versus the 4-4, checks the wing's block on the outside linebacker and helps him if needed. If no help is needed, arcs for the corner and makes the cornerback decide whether to cross the tackle's face. If he does, blocks him out. If not, keeps running to the corner. Versus the 5-3 with the end and wing double-teaming the end, blocks the outside linebacker.

Playside guard—Pulls and stays one yard behind and one yard deeper than the tackle. If the tackle hook blocks the outside linebacker, takes over the lead role of blocking the corner. If the tackle continues to convoy downfield, stays with him until he blocks, then moves up and takes the lead.

Fullback—Runs the 33/34 Delay. Uses crossover and plant steps and fakes like he has the ball.

Quarterback—Reverse pivots and leads the halfback with the pitch. Just tosses it, doesn't spin it. Then, hand fakes a give to the fullback on a delay.

Blocking ends—Versus the 4-3, reads whether the defensive end is crashing the C gap or hitting and reacting. If crashing, aims in front of the defensive end to get the head across his bow. If hitting and reacting, fires into the defensive end with the head outside of him. Versus the 5-2 and 5-3, the end and wing slot will double the defensive end, with the outside blocker having his head to the outside. Versus outside linebackers, anticipates a defensive reaction to the outside and aim outside of the linebacker's aligned spot. Then, adjusts the angle to engage the outside linebacker with the head on the outside. Be firm, but under control. Keeps the feet moving and tries to sustain the block. If the outside linebacker slips off the block, doesn't turn out and chases him. Looks at the safety and the inside linebackers and engages the next defensive threat.

Strongside Pitch

Refer to Figures 8-1 and 8-2.

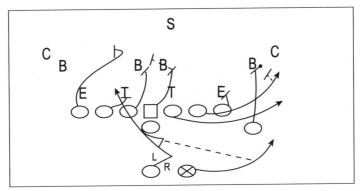

Figure 8-1. Sword White Pitch Right versus 4-4

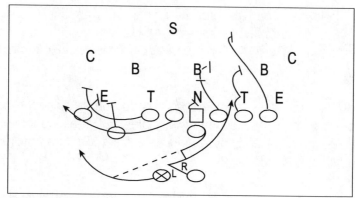

Figure 8-2. Lou White Pitch Left versus 5-3

Weakside Pitch

Examples of weakside pitch are shown in Figures 8-3 and 8-4. Refer to Figures 8-5 and 8-6 for examples of weakside pitch with crack motion.

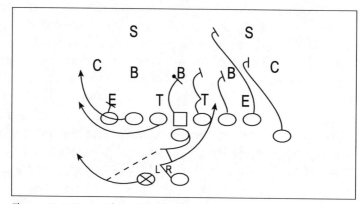

Figure 8-3. Ram White Pitch Left versus 4-3

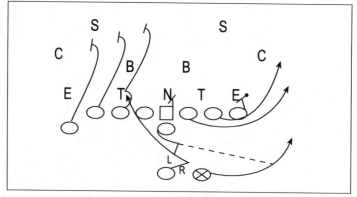

Figure 8-4. Lion White Pitch Right versus 5-2 (Note: to run the weakside pitch versus a 5 end, the defensive end needs to reduce to at least an outside eye or head up alignment.)

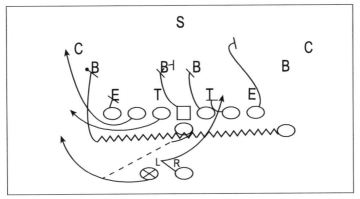

Figure 8-5. Sword Crack White Pitch Left versus 4-4

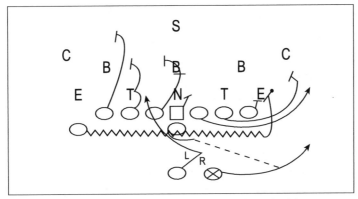

Figure 8-6. Lion Crack White Pitch Right with a double-team on the defensive end versus 5-3

Versus a defense that runs a defender across with the wingback motion, use Mo, which is a quick fullback motion to get the needed blocking at the perimeter. It is possible the defense will move an inside linebacker with him, but this move would weaken their inside defense, and most defensive coordinators will be reluctant to do so.

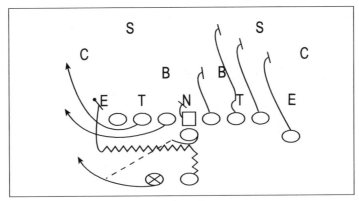

Figure 8-7. Ram Mo White Pitch Left versus 5-2

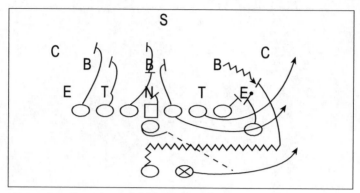

Figure 8-8. Sword Mo White Pitch Right versus 5-3

In summary, defenses will try to take away the pitch with one or more of the following strategies:

- Play the outside linebackers or cornerbacks closer to the line of scrimmage and fire up rapidly.
- Overshift to the strongside.
- Go man coverage and move the safety over and up to cover the inside receiver (tight end or slot).

To combat the first situation, the pulling linemen should block out on the firing defenders and the halfback will be ready to cut in, then go back out. To combat the second situation, attack the area the defense has weakened by their shift, plus pitch weak. To combat the third situation, run the pitch weak with Mo motion. To fully exploit these three defensive strategies, it is necessary to have companion misdirection plays, like the White Tackle Trap and the White Fullback Delay.

Tackle Trap

The quarterback makes a vigorous fake pitch with the ball, then an inside handoff to the slot/wing.

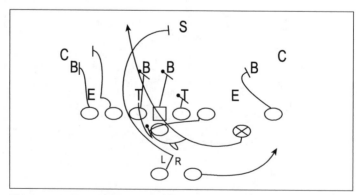

Figure 8-9. Rex White 41 Tackle Trap versus 4-4

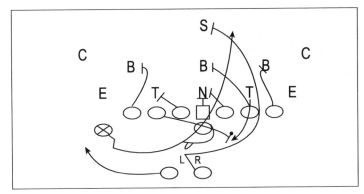

Figure 8-10. Lance White 42 Tackle Trap versus 5-3

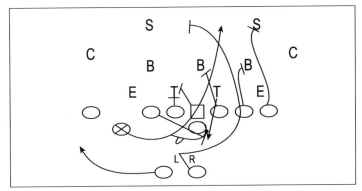

Figure 8-11. Lou White 42 Tackle Trap versus 4-3

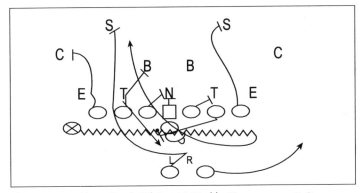

Figure 8-12. Lion Crack White 41 Tackle Trap versus 5-2

Fullback Delay

Generally, fold blocks are used, which are the opposite of the cross block. On the fold block, the inside lineman goes first and blocks out. The outside lineman steps back with his inside foot, then blocks a linebacker. However, a cross block is usually used versus the 4-4. Also, a trap scheme is good versus the 5-2 or 5-3. Therefore, it is best to just call the numbers and the blocking scheme and eliminate the word "delay." All players should know that when the fullback carries in White it's the delay. The fullback will take a crossover step, a plant step, and then aims at the guard's original position. This fact applies to all White delays, whether they are X, 33/34 Fold, or 35/36 Fold.

On the 3/4 Fold, the guard and tackle are the linemen on either side of those holes, so they fold. On the 5/6 Fold, the tackle and ends are the linemen on either side of those holes, so they fold.

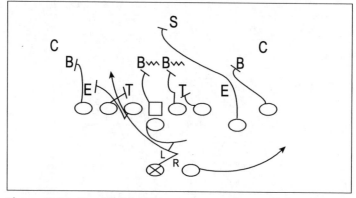

Figure 8-13. Rex White 33X versus 4-4 (Note: if the playside defensive tackle aligns in the A gap, the guard calls, "Base," and blocks the defensive tackle and the tackle blocks the defensive end.)

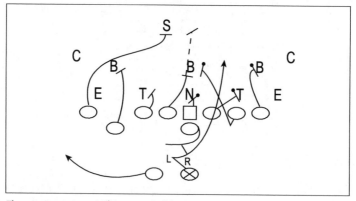

Figure 8-14. Lou White 34 Fold versus 5-3

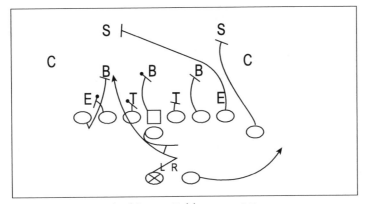

Figure 8-15. Sword White 35 Fold versus 4-3

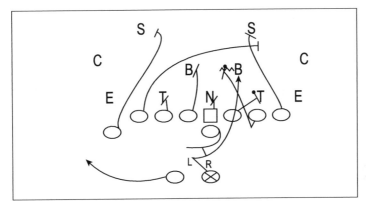

Figure 8-16. Lance White 34 Fold versus 5-2

White Banana Pass

Banana Pass is designed to be a 12 to 15-yard high-percentage pass. Maximum pass protection is employed with the line blocking area and the fullback and slot blocking the ends. The quarterback makes an aggressive pitch fake, gets more depth than when pitching, and then hops back a step. He reads both ends and throws to the most open receiver. The ends explode out at 45 degrees then curve back inside. They try to be over their original alignment, yet at 10 to 12-yard depth.

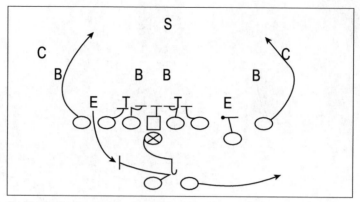

Figure 8-17. Rex White Banana Pass versus 4-4

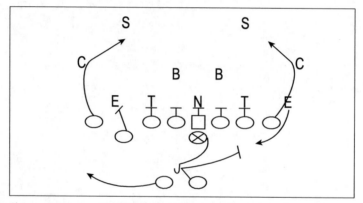

Figure 8-18. Lou White Banana Pass versus 5-2

9

Gray Series

The Gray series is a speed option series with only three plays. Short but sweet is a good description. The fullback, who aligns behind the quarterback, is the pitchback. The halfback, who aligns in the guard tackle gap, is the lead blocker. For this series to be effective, the fullback should have good speed and the ability to catch the pitch. If not, exchange positions with the fullback and halfback or align in the I. If the backs exchange positions, other times should exist when they exchange so this maneuver doesn't become a scouting tendency. The quarterback takes a large 45-degree step back toward the playside. He then angles toward the 5/6 hole at half speed to give him time to make the decision to keep or pitch. Like White Pitch, the Gray option can be run from several formations and with or without motion.

All diagrams show the quarterback pitching. However, if the defender being optioned plays the pitch, the quarterback will keep and run through the off-tackle area. This option play is very fast and hits outside quickly like the White Pitch.

Gray Option

Refer to Figures 9-1 through 9-4.

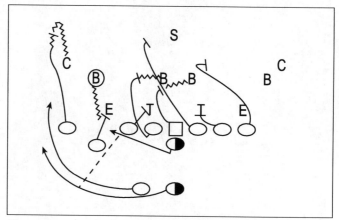

Figure 9-1. Lou Gray Option Left-B (to the strongside) versus 4-4

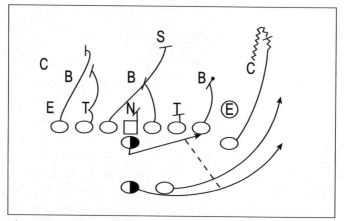

Figure 9-2. Sword Gray Option Right-E (to the strongside) versus 5-3

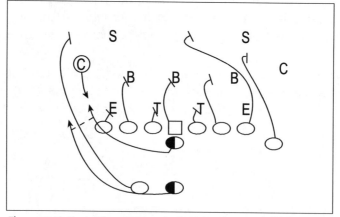

Figure 9-3. Ram Gray Option Left-C (to the weakside) versus 4-3

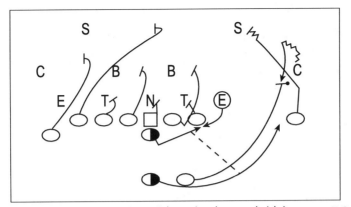

Figure 9-4. L Gray Option Right-E (to the weakside) versus 5-2

41/42 Tackle Trap

The tackle trap coming back inside is good strategy when the defense overplays the option. The blocking schemes are the same as the tackle traps from the other series. The quarterback makes an inside handoff to the slot/wing.

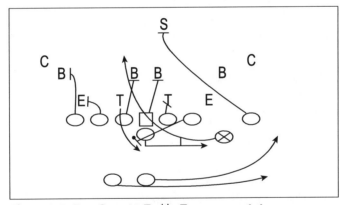

Figure 9-5. Rex Gray 41 Tackle Trap versus 4-4

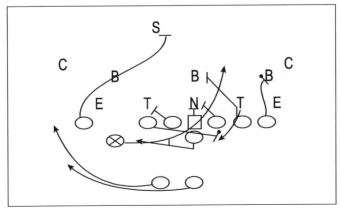

Figure 9-6. Lou Gray 42 Tackle Trap versus 5-3

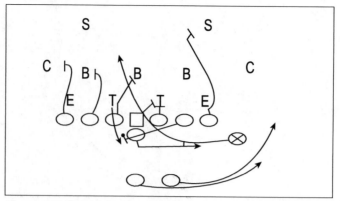

Figure 9-7. Sword Gray 41 Tackle Trap versus 4-3

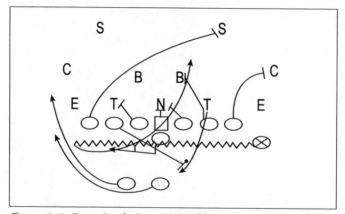

Figure 9-8. Ram Crack Gray 42 Tackle Trap versus 5-2

Gray Dump Pass

Versus three deep, the outside receivers run the dump route and, versus two deep, they run the hook route. The halfback becomes an outlet if the ends are covered. The

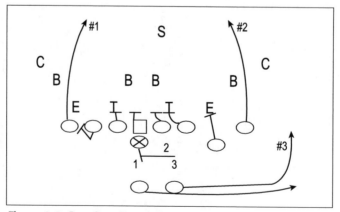

Figure 9-9. Rex Gray Dump Pass versus 4-4

quarterback shows option by holding the ball in front of his chest, but has his fingers on the laces. He stops on his third step, whirls around, and throws to #1 (backside end) if open. If not, he looks for #2. If #2 is not open, he throws to the outlet #3.

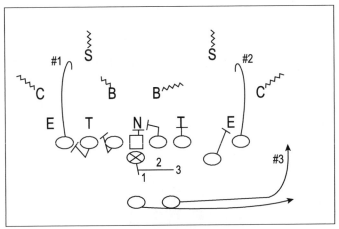

Figure 9-10. Rex Gray Hook Pass versus 5-2

10

Goal Line Offense–Brown Series

It is an advantage for the multiple offense to stay in regular formations until inside the five-yard line. This practice enables the offense to see the opponent's regular defense as long as possible. On the other hand, defenses will usually switch to their goal line defense inside the five-yard line. This combination of factors necessitates the implementation of a goal line offense.

The full house T formation, with two tight ends and three backs in the backfield, is called jumbo, and the plays run from jumbo are the Brown series. The fullback picks his depth based on his experience and quickness hitting the hole. The halfbacks align with their heels even with the fullback's toes and in the guard-tackle gap. Most defenses use a six-man line with five defenders at linebacker depth (6-5). Some teams that normally use a 5-3 or 5-2 defense will use a double eagle front with a seven-man line and four defenders at linebacker depth (7-4).

- The advantages of using jumbo and the Brown series on the goal line include:
- The fullback's greater size and power can result in positive yardage with runs between the tackles.
- The halfbacks are close to the line of scrimmage and can block the inside linebackers quickly.
- The fake handoff to the fullback will set up successful crossbuck, option, and play-action passes.

Brown Blast versus the 6-5

Since the fullback is right behind the quarterback, the quarterback should step back with his playside foot to avoid getting in the fullback's path. Versus the 6-5, the center always double-teams the playside nose. The backside guard will drive almost straight inside to prevent penetration by the backside nose. The tight end will block the man in or over the C gap.

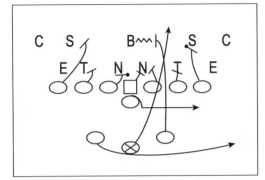

Figure 10-1. Jumbo Brown 34 Blast versus 6-5

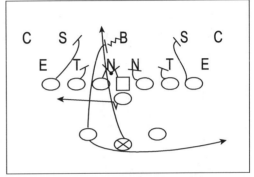

Figure 10-2. Jumbo Brown 33 Blast versus 6-5

Brown Tackle versus the 6-5

Brown Tackle is a good play when the defensive tackles start pinching to stop Brown Blast. The tackle drive blocks the pinching defensive tackle. The center blocks the playside gap with the playside guard. The tight end blocks the C gap. The halfback runs an inside out course and blocks out on the defensive end. The fullback aims at the tackle's inside foot and runs as tight a route as possible.

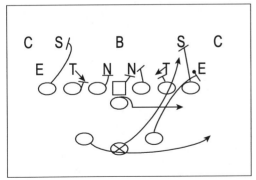

Figure 10-3. Jumbo Brown Right Tackle versus 6-5

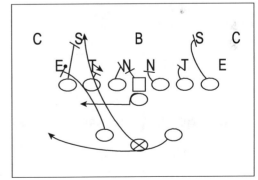

Figure 10-4. Jumbo Brown Left Tackle versus 6-5

Brown Belly versus the 6-5

Brown Belly is blocked the same as RT/LT Tackle, and the backfield action is the same as the Red Belly. The fake to the fullback, who is the primary ballcarrier on the goal line, adds significant deception to this play.

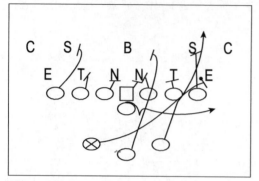

Figure 10-5. Jumbo Brown 26 Belly versus 6-5

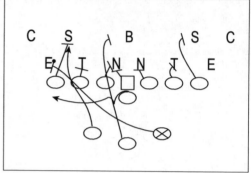

Figure 10-6. Jumbo Brown 45 Belly versus 6-5

Brown Cross Buck versus the 6-5

Brown Cross Buck is blocked the same as RT/LT Tackle and Belly RT/LT. Neither halfback hesitates or jab steps. Like Belly, the fake to the fullback deceives the defense plus gets them moving in the wrong direction.

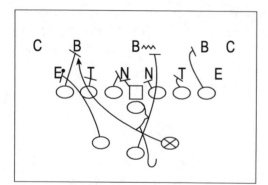

Figure 10-7. Jumbo Brown 45 Cross Buck versus 6-5

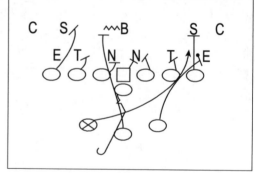

Figure 10-8. Jumbo Brown 26 Cross Buck versus 6-5

Brown Cross Option versus the 6-5

The Cross Option eliminates the middle linebacker from pursuit, plus it allows the pitchback to get into a better pitch relationship with the quarterback. While the regular option is a good play, goal line defenses have to react quicker to flow than they do in the open field. Thus, cross option is a hard play for a backed-up defense to stop.

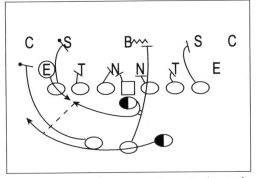

Figure 10-9. Jumbo Brown Cross Option Left-E versus 6-5

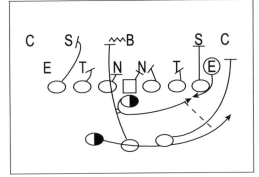

Figure 10-10. Jumbo Brown Cross Option Right-E versus 6-5

Brown 30 Fan versus the 7-4

The center blocks the nose tackle any way he wants to go. The guards and tackles fan block. The halfbacks cheat inside on alignment and block the linebackers. The fullback reads the center's block on the nose tackle and runs to daylight. The quarterback uses a midline technique to pivot out of the way and hands off to the fullback.

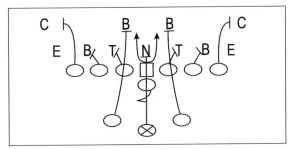

Figure 10-11. Jumbo Brown 30 Fan versus 7-4

Brown 30 Wedge versus the 7-4

Wedge blocking is always good in short-yardage situations. Refer to Figures 10-12 and 10-13.

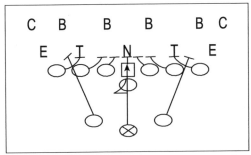

Figure 10-12. Jumbo Brown 30 Wedge versus 5-6

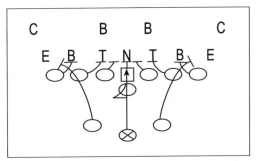

Figure 10-13. Jumbo Brown 30 Wedge versus 7-4

Brown Belly versus the 7-4

Refer to Figures 10-14 and 10-15.

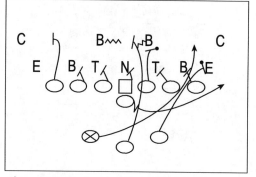

Figure 10-14. Jumbo Brown 26 Belly versus 7-4

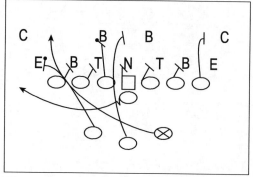

Figure 10-15. Jumbo Brown 45 Belly versus 7-4

Brown Crossbuck G versus the 7-4

Refer to Figures 10-16 and 10-17. The playside halfback's assignment is to block the playside linebacker over him. If he blitzes A gap, the halfback must meet him in the hole. Otherwise, the halfback leads through the hole.

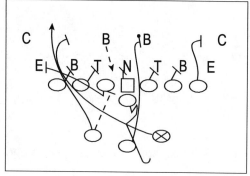

Figure 10-16. Jumbo Brown Cross Buck G versus 7-4 (Note: G means the tight end and tackle block down and the guard pulls and blocks out.)

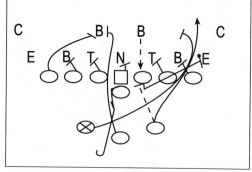

Figure 10-17. Jumbo Brown 26 Cross Buck G versus 7-4

Brown Cross Option versus the 7-4

Refer to Figures 10-18 and 10-19.

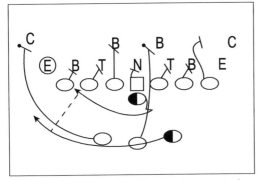

Figure 10-18. Jumbo Brown Cross Option Left-E versus 7-4

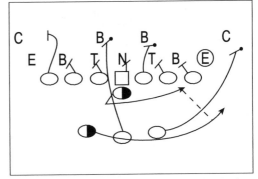

Figure 10-19. Jumbo Brown Cross Option Right-E versus 7-4

Brown Passes

These passes are universal and can be used versus any goal line defense. The playside halfback shows a block on the defensive end and then slides by him one-yard deep in the end zone. The fullback fakes LT/RT and then blocks the C gap to the defensive end. The backside halfback races over to help the fullback on the defensive end. The playside end aims seven-yards deep in the end zone.

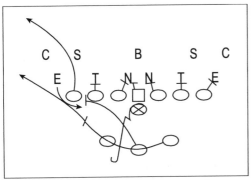

Figure 10-20. Jumbo Brown Pass Left versus 6-5

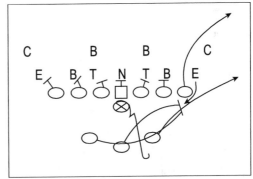

Figure 10-21. Jumbo Brown Pass Right versus 7-4

Brown Ends Cross

The direction call on cross tells the following: the fullback fakes over the callside guard. The callside halfback blocks the defensive end. The backside halfback runs two steps (crossover, plant) towards the callside, then turns back and blocks the defensive end. The tight end to the call runs an across route. The tight end away from the call runs an across route and goes under the other tight end. The quarterback reads both tight ends and throws to the open receiver.

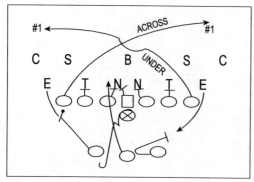

Figure 10-22. Jumbo Brown Ends Cross Left versus 6-5

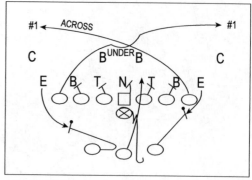

Figure 10-23. Jumbo Brown Ends Cross Right versus 7-4

Brown Pop Pass

The quarterback steps almost straight back and fakes to the fullback. He then scans the tight ends, rises on his toes, and throws a firm dart-like pass to the open man. If the tight ends have a linebacker/safety over them, they should approach him and fake a block with their hands, then burst by him on a skinny post. If no one is over them, they should run a peel route (tiny banana route). The callside halfback blocks the defensive end. The backside halfback fakes option to the callside.

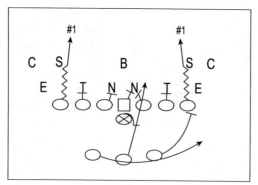

Figure 10-24. Jumbo Brown Pop Pass Right versus 6-5

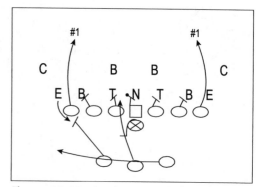

Figure 10-25. Jumbo Brown Pop Pass Left versus 7-4

11

The Come-from-Behind Offense

This situation dictates a formation that will spread the field, but, at the same time, places two backs in the backfield with the quarterback to run blasts and misdirection plays. The East/West formations spread the field, but keep two backs in the backfield with the quarterback. East means slot right, and West means slot left, as East on a map is always on the right side and West is on the left.

Following is a list of the plays that fit East/West. Because most of these plays have been diagramed in previous chapters, only the plays that have to be modified or are specific to East/West will be diagrammed in this chapter. These plays are denoted with an asterisk in the following list.

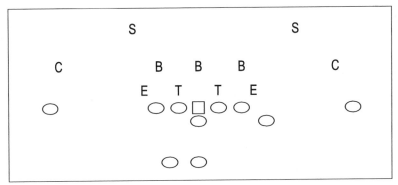

Figure 11-1. East formation versus 4-3

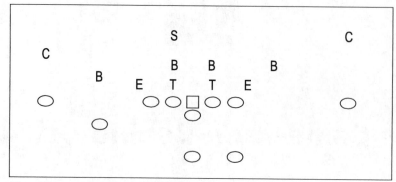

Figure 11-2. West formation versus 4-4

East/West Running Plays and Play-Action Passes

East/West Black 32/31 Trap
East/West Black 28/27 Sweep
East/West Black Bootleg LT/RT
East/West Black Screen RT/LT
East or West Black 30 Wedge
East/West Black 26/25 Trap
East/West Black Boot LT/RT
East/West Black Boot LT/RT Switch

East/West Kick Blue 33/34 Blast
East/West Crack Blue 42/41 Tackle Trap
East/West Crack Blue LT/RT-4 Wheel
East/West Crack Blue Pass LT/RT-Fade
*East/West Crack Blue 33/34X
East/West Crack Blue 44/43 Punch
East/West Crack Blue Pass LT/RT
East/West Crack Blue Pass LT/RT-Skinny
East/West Crack Blue Pass LT/RT-Flood

East/West Green 34/33X
*East/West Green 43/44 Punch (Fake 34/33)
East/West Green Option RT/LT-E
East/West Green Pass RT/LT
East/West Red 34/33 Dive
East/West Red 26/25 Belly

East/West Red 26/25 Keep
East/West Red Option RT/LT-C
*East/West Red 43/44 Punch (Fake 34/33)
*East/West Red 34/33 Slant Pass
East/West Kick Red 23/24 Dive
East/West Crack Red 35/36 Belly
East/West Crack Red 35/36 Keep
East/West Crack Red Option LT/RT-C
*East/West Crack Red 44/43 Punch (Fake 23/24)
*East/West Crack Red 23/24 Slant Pass

*East/West Crack Orange 24/34X
*East/West Crack Orange Pass LT/RT
*East/West Crack Orange Bootleg RT/LT

East/West Crack White Pitch LT/RT
East/West Crack White 42/41 Tackle Trap
East/West Crack White Slant Pass LT/RT
East/West Mo White Pitch LT/RT
East/West Crack White 34/33X

East/West Gray Option LT/RT-E
East/West Crack Gray 42/41 Tackle Trap
East/West Crack Gray Option LT/RT-E
East/West Crack Gray Slant Pass LT/RT

Note: Banana patterns in Red and White and the dump pattern in Gray are replaced by slant patterns due to the width of the receivers.

43/44 Punch

Punch is a trap play without the usual double-team inside the hole. Thus, it is base blocking with the backside guard pulling across and blocking the first defender outside the hole called. Base blocking is used because with the ends split not all the defenders at the point of attack can be blocked if the line were to double-team the first defender inside the hole. The quarterback fakes an inside handoff, hands off to the slot, then fakes per the color series called.

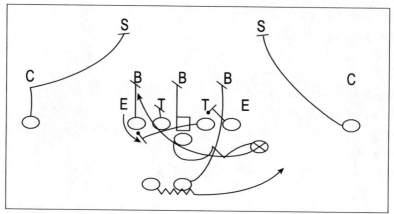

Figure 11-3. East Green 43 Punch versus 4-3 (Note: the quarterback fakes 34, hands off, and fakes green option.)

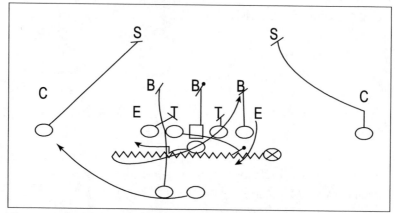

Figure 11-4. East Crack Red 44 Punch versus 4-3 (Note: the quarterback fakes 23, hands off, and fakes red option.)

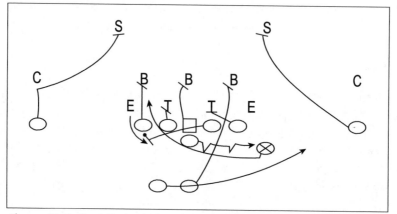

Figure 11-5. East Red 43 Punch versus 4-3 (Note: the quarterback fakes 34, hands off, and fakes red option.)

Slant Pass

Refer to Figures 11-6 and 11-7.

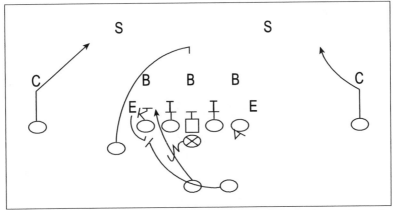

Figure 11-6. West Red 33 Slant Pass versus 4-3 (Note: the 33/34 tells the backs which way to play action.)

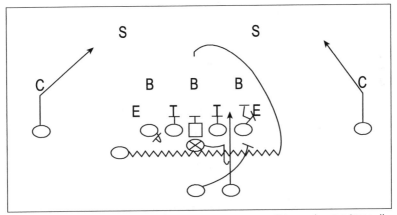

Figure 11-7. West Crack 24 Slant Pass versus 4-3 (Note: the 24/23 tells the backs which way to play action.)

Crack Orange Plays

Refer to Figures 11-8 through 11-10.

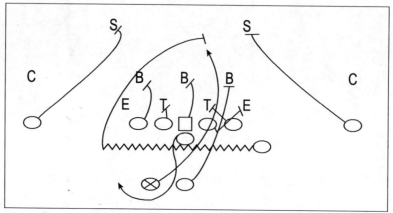

Figure 11-8. East Crack Orange 24X versus 4-3

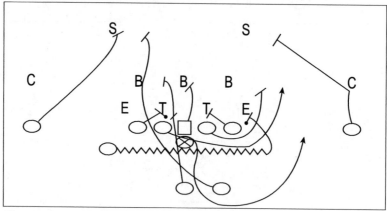

Figure 11-9. West Crack Orange Bootleg Right versus 4-3

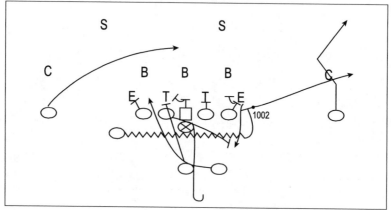

Figure 11-10. West Crack Orange Pass Right versus 4-3

21/22 Lead Draw

The quarterback should backpedal three steps before turning and handing off to the halfback. The halfback shows pass blocking, while shuffling inside to take the handoff.

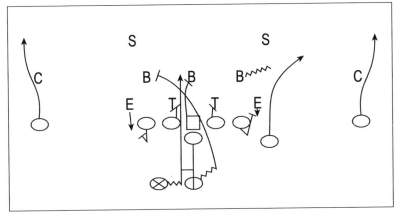

Figure 11-11. East 21 Lead Draw versus 4-3

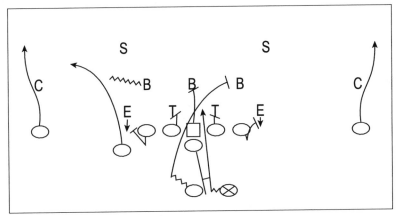

Figure 11-12. West 22 Lead Draw versus 4-3

Tan Series—Three-Step Dropback Pass Series

For simplicity, only the East formation will be diagrammed. But, all the pass plays should be learned from both East and West so that the slot can be aligned to the wideside of the field. Big-on-big blocking is used on all Tan passes. The center has the middle linebacker if he blitzes. The fullback checks the linebacker on his side and then swings as an outlet receiver to the slotside. The halfback does the same to the weakside. The slot's basic route is a slant through the middle versus two deep and an across route underneath the safety versus three deep. The split ends align with the inside foot forward.

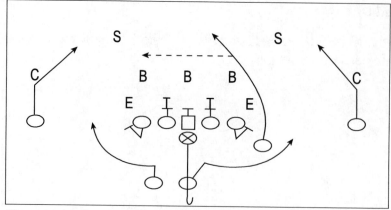

Figure 11-13. East Tan Slant versus 4-3 (Note: the split ends run three-step slants.)

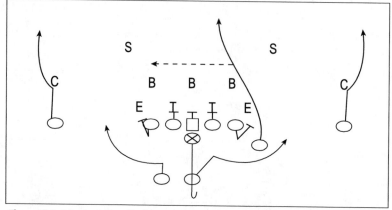

Figure 11-14. East Tan Fade versus 4-3 (Note: the split ends run vertical for four steps, then arc out and look over their inside shoulder.)

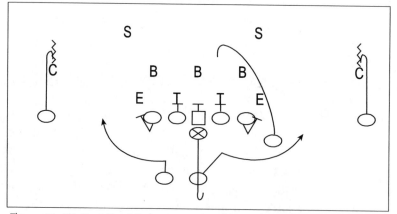

Figure 11-15. East Tan Hitch versus 4-3 (Note: the split ends run a five-step stop route. The slot runs a seven-step inside hitch route.)

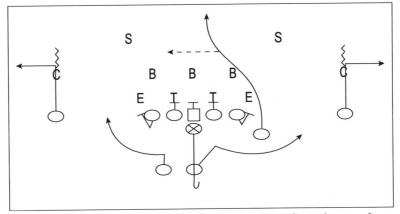

Figure 11-16. East Tan Out versus 4-3 (Note: the split ends run a four-step out route.)

Gold Series—Five-Step Dropback Pass Series

Figures 11-17 through 11-19 illustrate three pass patterns that time up better with a five-step dropback, including a deep out, a hook, and a hitch and go. Gold pass protection is the same as Tan. For simplicity, they will only be diagrammed from West.

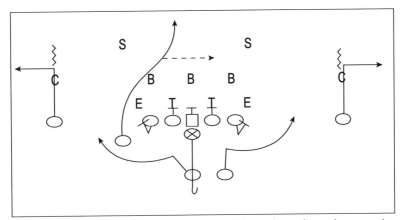

Figure 11-17. West Gold Out versus 4-3 (Note: the split ends run a six-step out route.)

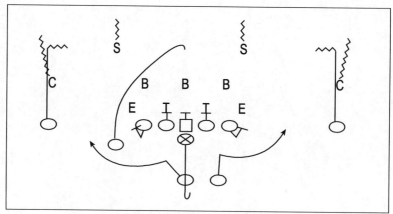

Figure 11-18. West Gold Hook versus 4-3 (Note: the split ends run a seven-step hook route. The slot runs a nine-step hook route.)

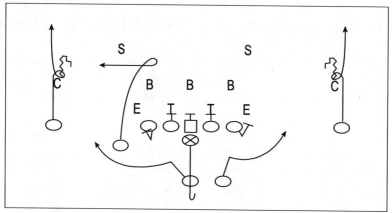

Figure 11-19. West Gold Hook and Go versus 4-3 (Note: the split ends run a five hard hitch and go route. The slot runs a seven-step hitch and out route.)

12

The I Formation in the Multiple Offense

The I formation has a place in the multiple offense when a halfback with speed and toughness is matched with a big and strong offensive line. No new series are needed because plays can be selected from the series that best fit the I formation. Two new I formations are used: I Flanker (Right/Left) and I Slot (Rip/Liz).

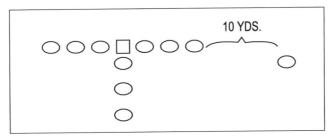

Figure 12-1. I Right

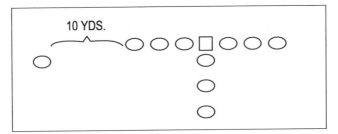

Figure 12-2. I Left

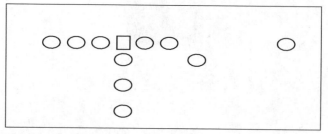

Figure 12-3. I Rip

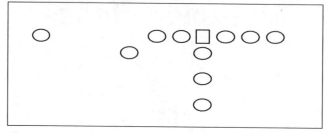

Figure 12-4. I Liz

Right/Left and Rip/Liz are similar formations. A good blocking slotback in Rip/Liz can serve most of the same functions as the flanker side tight end in Right/Left. And, essentially no difference exists between the split end of Rip/Liz and the flanker of Right/Left. The slotback in Rip/Liz can run counter and tackle trap plays, plus motion across for blocking and pass receiving.

The double tight end set of Right/Left allows the offense to run mirrored (identical) plays to each side, plus greater power blocking behind the flanker side tight end. By using the word trade, it is possible to get motion from the flanker side tight end in Right/Left. Trade tells the flanker to shift forward and become a split end and the tight end to step back and become a slot. Then, the tight end is just like the slotback in Rip/Liz.

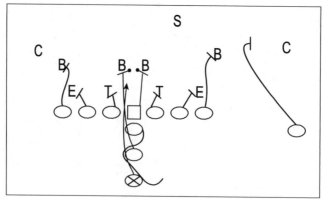

Figure 12-5. I Right Orange 21 Fan versus 4-4

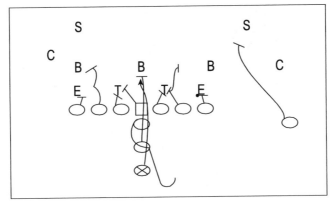

Figure 12-6. I Right Orange 22 Blast versus 4-3

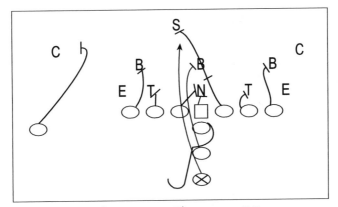

Figure 12-7. I Left Orange 21 Blast versus 5-3

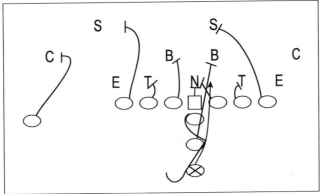

Figure 12-8. I Left Orange 22 Blast versus 5-2

23/24X

23/24X is only run versus the 4-4 and 4-3. Also, 23/24X can be run toward either tight end. The quarterback should drop back to the two-receiver side after the handoff.

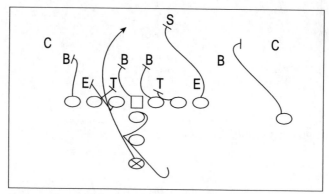

Figure 12-9. I Right Orange 23X versus 4-4

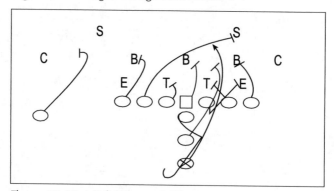

Figure 12-10. I Left Orange 24X versus 4-3

25/26 Power

Refer to Figures 12-11 and 12-12.

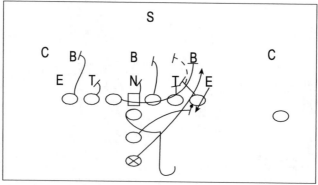

Figure 12-11. I Right Orange 26 Power versus 5-3 (Note: the 25/26 Power is only run versus the 5-3 and 5-2.)

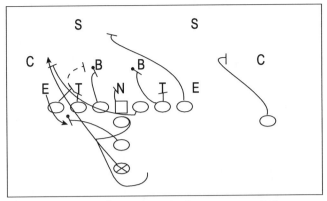

Figure 12-12. I Right Orange 25 Power versus 5-2

Orange Pass Right/Left

Refer to Figures 12-13 and 12-14.

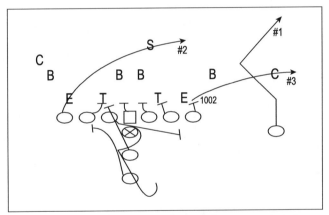

Figure 12-13. I Right Orange Pass Right versus 4-4 three deep

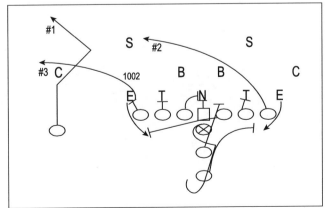

Figure 12-14. I Left Orange Pass Left versus 5-2 two deep

31/32 Dive

The quarterback's footwork is like the midline dive. On all Red 31/32 dives, the fullback aligns at three yards depth and the tailback aligns two yards behind the fullback.

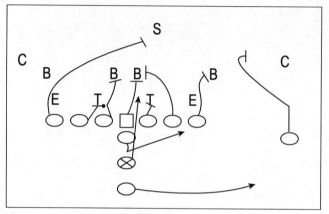

Figure 12-15. I Right Red 32 Dive versus 4-4

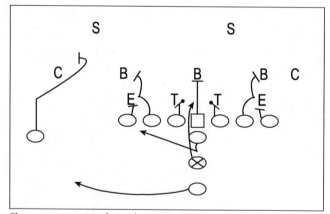

Figure 12-16. I Left Red 31 Dive versus 4-3

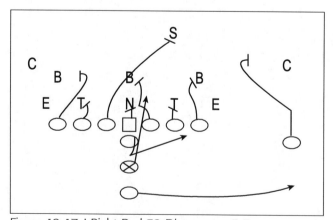

Figure 12-17. I Right Red 32 Dive versus 5-3

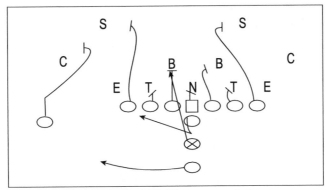

Figure 12-18. I Right Red 31 Dive versus 5-2

33/34X

Do not run 33/34X or Dive versus the 4-4 because one more defender than blockers exists.

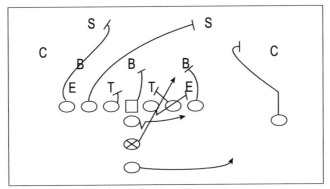

Figure 12-19. I Right Red 34X versus 4-3

Tackle

Run Tackle versus the 5-3 and 5-2 only. The fullback runs off the tackle's block.

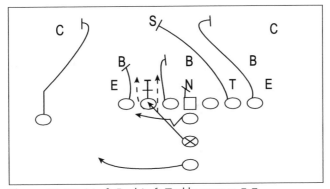

Figure 12-20. I Left Red Left Tackle versus 5-3

Red Option

Refer to Figures 12-21 through 12-24.

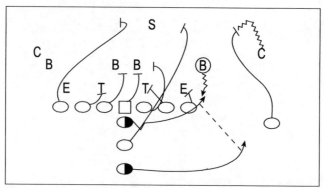

Figure 12-21. I Right Red Option Right-B versus 4-4

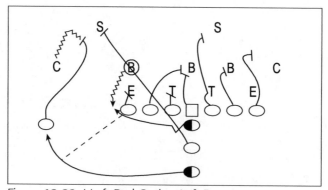

Figure 12-22. I Left Red Option Left-B versus 4-3

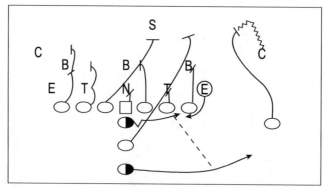

Figure 12-23. I Right Red Option Right-E versus 5-3

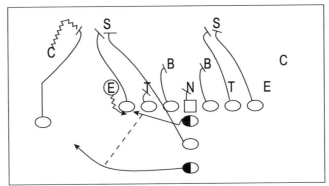

Figure 12-24. I Left Red Option Left-E versus 5-2

25/26 Counter and Red Counter Pass

The blocking is identical to all previous 45/46 Counters. The tailback's deeper alignment gives him a better view of blocking and potential running lanes. He takes three shuffle steps to the side of the fullback fake.

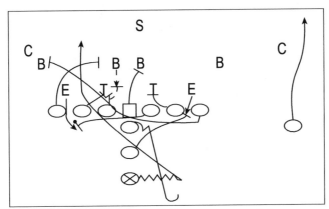

Figure 12-25. I Right Red 25 Counter versus 4-4

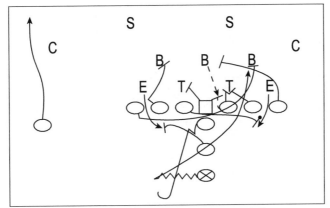

Figure 12-26. I Left Red 26 Counter versus 4-3

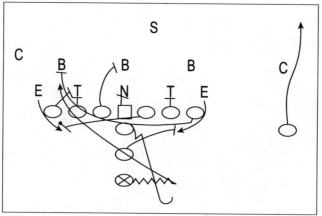

Figure 12-27. I Right Red 25 Counter versus 5-3

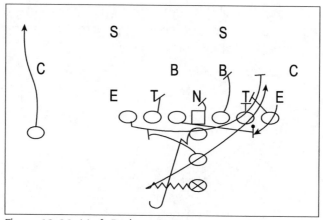

Figure 12-28. I Left Red 26 Counter versus 5-2

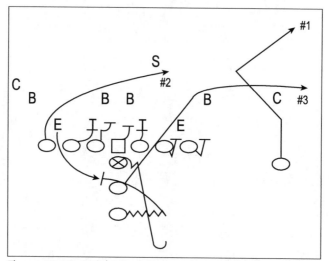

Figure 12-29. I Right Red Counter Pass Right versus 4-4

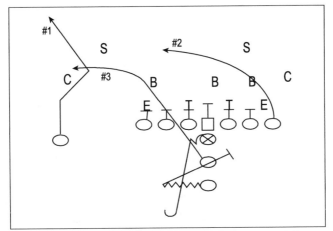

Figure 12-30. I Left Red Counter Pass Left versus 4-3

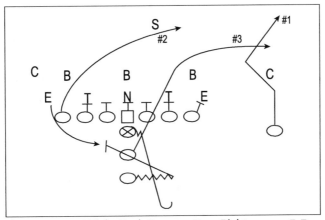

Figure 12-31. I Right Red Counter Pass Right versus 5-3

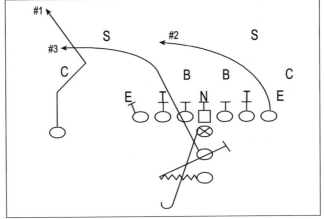

Figure 12-32. I Left Red Counter Pass Left versus 5-2

Gray Option

Refer to Figures 12-33 through 12-36.

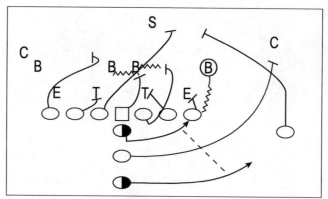

Figure 12-33. I Right Gray Option Right-B versus 4-4

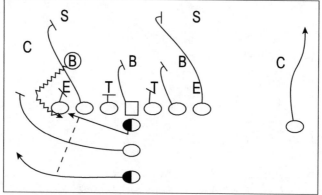

Figure 12-34. I Right Gray Option Left-B versus 4-3

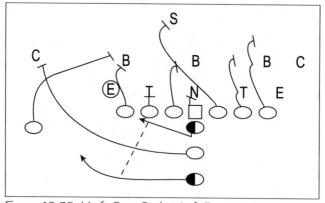

Figure 12-35. I Left Gray Option Left-E versus 5-3

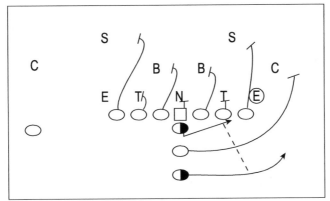

Figure 12-36. I Left Gray Option Right-E versus 5-2

Gray Passes

Refer to Figures 12-37 and 12-38.

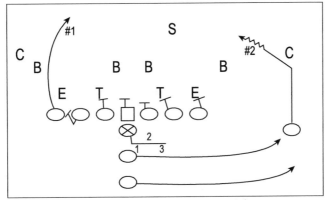

Figure 12-37. I Right Gray Dump Pass Right versus 4-4 (Note: the flanker runs at the cornerback and fakes a stalk block, then runs a slant pattern.)

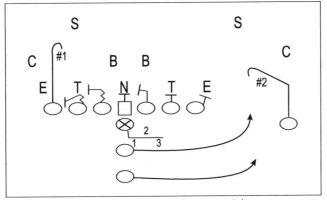

Figure 12-38. I Right Gray Hook Pass Right versus 5-2 (Note: the flanker runs a three-step slant and then hooks after three more steps.)

Sprint Pass Right/Left

The Sprint Right series consists of five semi-sprint pass plays. The quarterback sets up to throw behind the tackle and tight area.

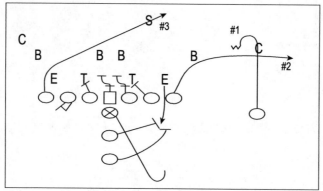

Figure 12-39. I Right Sprint Pass Right, Curl versus 4-4

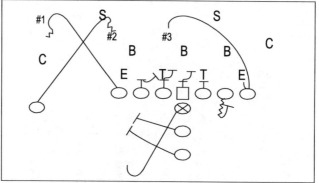

Figure 12-40. I Left Sprint Pass Left, X Hooks versus 4-3 (Note: X means flanker and nearest tight end cross routes [angle in and out], then hook.)

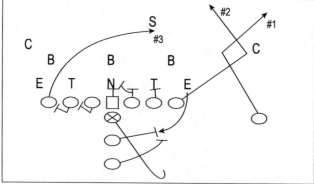

Figure 12-41. I Right Sprint Pass Right, V's versus 5-3 (Note: V's mean flanker and nearest tight end cross routes by angling, then re-cross as shown.)

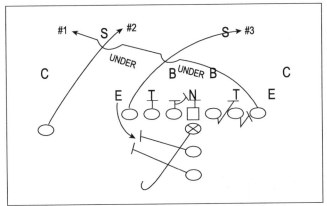

Figure 12-42. I Left Sprint Pass Left, Ends Cross versus 5-2 (Note: the tight ends cross with the end away from the call going underneath the call end's route. The split end angles in to provide a second crossing action.)

Sprint Tight End Screen

The Flood Pass to the strongside is faked. The quarterback sprints deeper, scans the dummy receivers, then turns and slightly leads the tight end so he has forward momentum. The tight end, tackle, guard, and center must all block hard for two counts before releasing to block. The tight end must force the defensive end to rush wide and then slip behind him and set up.

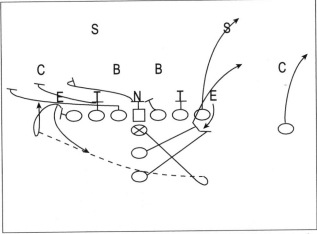

Figure 12-43. I Right Sprint Right, Tight End Screen Left versus 5-2

Rip/Liz Plays

Figures 12-44 through 12-53 illustrate the differences that exist between Right/Left and Rip/Liz formations.

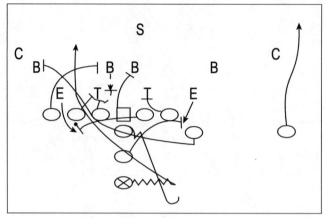

Figure 12-44. I Rip Red 25 Counter versus 4-4 (Note: the slot becomes the lead through the hole blocker, stepping back with the inside foot and going behind the fullback's fake.)

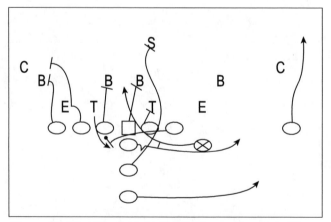

Figure 12-45. I Rip Red 41 Tackle Trap versus 4-4 (Note: the blocking is identical to all previous 41/42 Tackle Traps. The quarterback makes inside handoff to the slotback.)

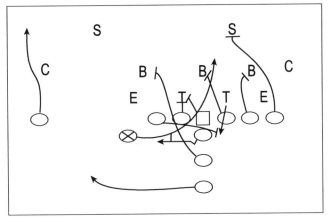

Figure 12-46. I Liz Red 42 Tackle Trap versus 4-3

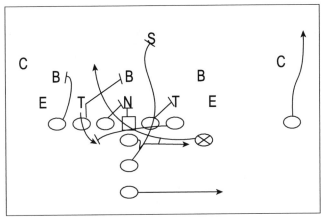

Figure 12-47. I Rip Red 41 Tackle Trap versus 5-3

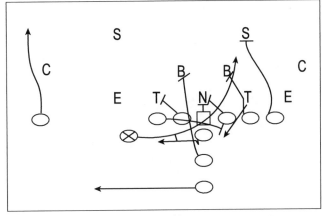

Figure 12-48. I Liz Red 42 Tackle Trap versus 5-2

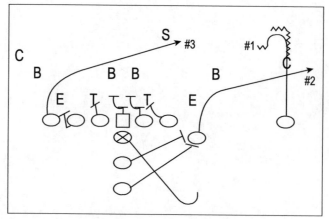

Figure 12-49. I Rip Sprint Pass Right, Curl versus 4-4

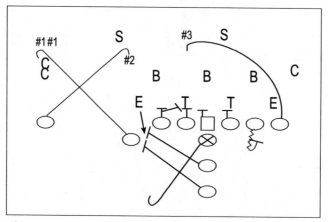

Figure 12-50. I Liz Sprint Pass Left, X Hook versus 4-3

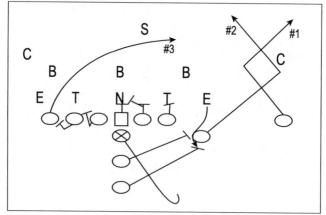

Figure 12-51. I Rip Sprint Pass Right, V's versus 5-3

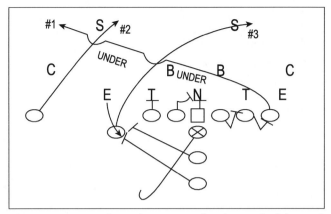

Figure 12-52. I Liz Sprint Pass Left, Slot and Tight End Cross versus 5-2

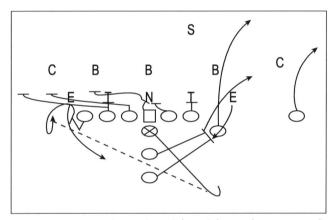

Figure 12-53. I Rip Sprint Right, Tight End Screen Left versus 5-3

Other I Rip/Liz Plays

Due to the similarities between Right/Left and Rip/Liz, diagrams are not provided for the following plays:

Orange 21/22 Fan (versus 4-4)

Orange 21/22 Blast (versus 4-3, 5-2, and 5-3)

Orange 23/24X (versus 4-3 and 4-4)

Orange 25/26 Power to tight end's side (versus 5-2 and 5-3)

Orange 25/26 Power to slot side (versus 5-2 and 5-3) (slot combos with tackle to the linebacker)

Orange Pass

Red 31/32 Dive (versus all defenses)

Red 33/34X (versus 4-3)

Red Right-Left Tackle (versus 5-2 and 5-3)

Red Option RT/LT (versus 4-3 and 4-4)

Red Option RT/LT (versus 5-3 and 5-2)

Red Counter Pass RT/LT—slot stays in and blocks end (versus all defenses).

Gray Option RT/LT—If play towards him, slot blocks end versus 4-3 and 4-4, and blocks outside linebacker versus 5-3, and onside safety versus 5-2.

Gray Dump and Hook Pass—slot stays in and blocks end (versus all defenses).

About the Author

Chuck Shroyer is the offensive coordinator and offensive backs/outside linebackers coach at Lapel (IN) High School. Previously, he worked as offensive coordinator and backfield coach at Tippecanoe Valley High School in Akron-Mentone, Indiana. During Shroyer's two-year tenure (2000-2002), TVHS won 15 games and lost six, a significant boost over a near-.500 average for the previous five years.

Shroyer began coaching youth football in 1967. From 1974 through 1977, he also served as spotter/strategy analyst for Dakota Wesleyan University in Mitchell, South Dakota. In 1995, he finished his youth coaching career with a record of 175 wins, 49 losses, and four ties. During his last 16 years of youth coaching, Shroyer conducted season-long experiments with different offensive series and plays.

In 1995, Shroyer joined Southwood High School in Wabash, Indiana, as assistant offensive coordinator and backfield coach. In the five seasons he was there, Southwood won 43 games and lost 11. During those five years, their offense averaged 31.3 points per game, which far exceeded any previous period in the school's history.

Shroyer has an economics degree from DePauw University, an MBA from Ball State University, and two engineering degrees earned through 3M/1CS work study. He worked at 3M for more than 37 years, serving as a plant manager (at two different locations) for 23 of those years.